HOW MY DOG SAVED MY LIFE

HOW MY DOG SAVED MY LIFE

THIRTY TALES OF COURAGE AND COMPASSION

Cate Cochran

with illustrations by Roslyn Schwartz

Collins

An Imprint of HarperCollins*PublishersLtd*

How My Dog Saved My Life

Illustrations by Roslyn Schwartz.

Published by Collins, an imprint of HarperCollins Publishers Ltd

FIRST EDITION

This book draws on the experience of the author and her interviews with other dog owners. Some names and other details have been changed.

HarperCollins books may be purchased for educational, business, or sales promotional use through our Special Markets Department.

HarperCollins Publishers Ltd
Bay Adelaide Centre, East Tower
22 Adelaide Street West, 41st Floor
Toronto, Ontario, Canada
M5H 4E3
www.harpercollins.ca

HarperCollins Publishers
Macken House, 39/40 Mayor Street Upper
Dublin 1, D01 C9W8, Ireland
www.harpercollins.com

Library and Archives Canada Cataloguing in Publication information is available on request.

ISBN 978-1-4434-7133-6

Printed and bound in the United States of America

25 26 27 28 29 LBC 5 4 3 2 1

For Calvin

2012–2024

Contents

CONTENTS

HOW MY DOG SAVED MY LIFE

Moishie

Introduction

When I heard the words "release the hound," Moishie was the last thing I expected to see. Seconds later, a long-haired Dachshund, with coal-black eyes and a blond coat dusted with threads of black, sauntered into the room and plunked himself down beside the chair where I was waiting to have a complicated surgery.

My dentist had referred me to a specialist for a procedure that was going to require a long session, and I was rattled by the prospect. When I arrived for my appointment, Ginny Eidinger, an expert in oral and maxillofacial surgery, reassured me that I would feel no pain and everything was going to be fine. But, she said, I was welcome to have their "comfort dog" sit on my lap during the surgery.

I'd never heard of such a thing, but I am a dog person and I thought, "What the heck, why not?" At the appointed time, Dr. Eidinger called to her staff, and in came Moishie. She gave him to me, and he settled himself in my lap, where he remained for the duration of the procedure. Almost instantly I could feel myself relaxing. When Dr. Eidinger had completed her work and the staff began to put away the surgical tools, Moishie roused himself and jumped to the floor. Afterwards I asked her about this. "When the procedure is over, he knows. I don't know if it's that I say to the patient, 'It's all finished,' and he understands those words in his own dog way, but even if he's in a deep sleep, his head goes up, he looks at me and he's ready to jump down off the chair." I didn't know it then, but I'd had my first encounter with a support animal. While Moishie may not have been officially trained for the job, he is certainly attuned to the role of putting an apprehensive patient at ease. In my case, perhaps it was stroking his silky coat or that I tuned in to his gentle demeanour—whatever it was that day, it had a calming effect.

I was a radio producer at the time, and I became interested in making a documentary about how Moishie had helped other adults and children who were also nervous about getting into the chair. Dr. Eidinger told me that she'd started to bring Moishie into the office out of necessity when her dog walker quit. "It just evolved from there," she explained. "I have some very, very nervous patients with significant anxiety. It's difficult, what we do. Patients come in and we're causing pain." I was one of her easier patients, but some people find it almost impossible to settle themselves and are really antsy about opening their mouths for whatever procedure they need. "Moishie's response to them is to tuck into the patient's lap more deeply," Dr. Eidinger said. "He'll try and put his head on the patient's arm or hand to reassure them. He'll sometimes make a sighing noise. It's almost like he says to the patient, 'I understand. It's terrible, but I'm with you. I'll take you through this process. You're going to be okay!'"

When I did make that documentary for CBC Radio's *The Sunday Edition* in 2019, I was floored to hear the stories of how a little dog weighing all of fifteen pounds had been so helpful to nervous and sometimes frantically worried patients facing multiple invasive and unsettling procedures. One patient, for example, whose childhood dental experiences had been so negative they left her with a form of post-traumatic stress disorder (PTSD), had lingering and significant problems with her teeth and needed many treatments. She had been seeing Dr. Eidinger for a long time, and every session completely freaked her out. But when Moishie came on the scene and she had him on her lap, the procedure became manageable. As Dr. Eidinger so aptly put it, "Moishie was a pivotal part of her emotional rehabilitation, if you will." In that sense, Moishie has probably saved numerous lives over the years. At the very least, he has helped many people to negotiate their emotions long enough to have the necessary dental work done.

Moishie is just one example of how dogs key in to people's distress. Dogs are deeply empathetic and able to understand humans in ways that surpass language. Any dog owner knows how comforting it is to have their dog nuzzle them at just the right moment. And dogs act in ways that are, at times, astonishing—not only sensing danger, but actively finding ways to help in an emergency. They are now being trained to be highly sophisticated support and service dogs working with people who are blind, or deaf, or coping with grief, or living with autism, or surviving PTSD, or overcoming anger issues, or enduring life-threatening illnesses, or coping with anxiety and depression—

the list goes on. What is almost breathtaking is the way that when a dog and a person are paired up together, whether the dog is highly trained or just a plain mutt with a gift, the coupling expands the possibilities for individuals to live their lives independently.

The earliest known evidence of a support dog is seen on a mural in the ruins of the ancient Roman city Herculaneum, dating back to the first century AD. The mural depicts a man walking with a dog at the end of a leash. There's speculation that the man might be blind and is possibly being guided by the dog. While perhaps not a trained support dog, we can infer it was a dog loyal to the needs of its owner. The first formal program to train dogs to help blind people was at "Les Quinze-Vingts" hospital for the blind in Paris in 1780. Subsequently, guide dogs were trained to assist World War I vets who came home from the battlefields blinded, often by mustard gas. The first guide dog school in the world, The Seeing Eye, opened in New York in 1928. The term "service dog" came into common parlance when an American canine researcher, Bonnie Bergin, invented the term in the 1970s. Wanting to find a way to keep people out of institutions, she founded the first organization that trained dogs for people with disabilities in 1975. Since then, schools for support dogs have popped up all over the world. You'll meet some of these dogs in this book, and you'll also meet a trainer who has dealt with profound trauma himself and is training service dogs with virtuosic support skills. His dogs are so highly trained they are able to work with people with multiple complex needs.

Much ink has been spilled over the years about the enduring relationship between dogs and their owners, and why we are endlessly fascinated by them. This book, *How My Dog Saved*

My Life, is a collection of real-life (and sometimes stranger than fiction) accounts of dogs that have rescued their owners from grave injury or almost certain death—service dogs and guide dogs that protect their owners and keep them safe from peril in an ongoing way, and companion dogs that shore up those who deal with mental, emotional and/or physical disabilities.

In my professional life I have done many interviews, and I respect what a gift it is for people to share their stories. Each of the people in this book agreed to speak to me at length about intimate details of their own lives, in some cases sharing their story for the first time. I am grateful to each person for that. As I spoke to them, I kept feeling a sense of wonder about how they handle the challenges that have been thrown at them, often in catastrophic situations. The people you'll meet have, with the help of their canine friends, risen above myriad difficulties with grace, humility, and humour, and their resilience amazes me still. And as for the dogs, well, as people in the support and service world say, "They're not just pets, they're partners."

Buddy

Leading the Way

Some months ago, Alex (whose story is in this book) told me she was finally going to get her new Seeing Eye guide dog. She had waited a long, long time for this moment. It's not easy to get a guide dog, and over the last many years, she's been through several disastrous undertakings with some schools. When she mentioned she was going to New Jersey to get her dog, I was curious about this school I knew nothing about. As I started to do a little research, I realized it is the oldest school of its kind.

As it turns out, Alex was paired with Brody, an especially serene animal who is highly skilled at guiding Alex hither and yon. He accompanies her when she travels. Brody, who is a mid-size Black Lab, makes himself small enough to wiggle under her seat on the plane. He's already guided her on numerous other adventures, and together they make their way around the urban chaos in her city's downtown core.

I became curious about this school, The Seeing Eye. I began to do some research about it, and then I stumbled on this quote: "As I put my hand down on Buddy, I knew that she was going to be my Declaration of Independence and give me back the freedom that I so long desired to go and come as I please. And that she also would be the pioneer of the guide dog movement in the United States for the blind men and women who neither wanted charity nor pity but wanted to live a normal life with normal people."

Those are the words of Morris Frank, the first North American recipient of a guide dog. He was a New Yorker whose German Shepherd guide dog, Buddy, was trained by Dorothy Harrison Eustis, an American dog trainer living in Switzerland. Frank had written to Eustis when he was nineteen, after his father read him an article she had written for the *Saturday Evening Post* in 1927. The article, entitled "The Seeing Eye," resulted from a visit she had made to a school in Potsdam, Germany, that was training guide dogs for blind World War I veterans. In the article she noted, "It is little short of marvelous how a raw dog can be taken into the school and in four months be turned out a blind leader, and the miracle is that the dog so perfectly assimilates his instruction. From the very small beginnings of becoming housebroken, he is taken step by step upward to his life work of leading a blind man, of being that man's eyes and his sword and buckler."

Frank had his own remarkable story. His mother had become blind in two separate accidents, and he subsequently became blind in two accidents—one when he was horseback riding at the age of six and the second, a boxing accident when he was sixteen. Frank's father read Eustis's article to him, after which Frank sent her the letter. It said, in part, "Is what you say really true? If so, I want one of those dogs! And I am not alone. Thousands of blind like me abhor being dependent on others."

After his overture, Eustis agreed to give him a dog, Buddy, and train him to work with the dog; in 1928 Frank flew over to work with Eustis for a few months at her dog school in Switzerland. There is newsreel footage of him taking his first somewhat tentative steps. Recalling them, he later said, "As they showed me how to put the harness on the dog and we started down the road, as my legs stretched out, my shoulders went back, and my head went up and the wind blew in my face. I knew I had my independence."

Frank had promised Eustis that he would sing the praises of guide dogs, and he did. He and Buddy became a canine cause célèbre in the US when he flew home to New York in June of 1928. He spoke to a phalanx of reporters about the wonder of having a guide dog, demonstrating the point by navigating busy streets and crossings. Afterward Frank sent Eustis a one-word telegram about how his public relations efforts had paid off: "Success."

When Eustis moved back to the US the following year, she and Frank set up the first guide dog school in North America, calling it The Seeing Eye; it is now the oldest existing guide dog school in the world. Their mission was to train service dogs that would help make an inaccessible world accessible to visually impaired people and eventually to people with other disabilities.

In 1931, Eustis trained four guide dogs for a British undertaking by two British women, which led to the founding of a guide dog association in the UK. There are dozens of schools around the world now, many of which have branched out into training dogs for differing access and support needs.

The first Canadian school for guide dogs opened in Quebec in 1981. Today the need for dogs far outstrips their availability. According to the Canadian National Institute for the Blind, "In order to obtain a guide dog in a reasonable timeframe, many Canadians end up getting their dogs from US-based schools."

Wait times are frustrating, and it is expensive and time-consuming to train skilled guide dogs. Matching a person with the right dog is not an exact science, but when it works, these impressive animals open the world to their owners, helping them live more fully realized lives.

The Nose Knows

I have two dogs who love nothing more than taking a leisurely walk through our neighbourhood. Before I started working on this book, there were times when I found their meanderings frustrating. The dogs would dilly-dally, seemingly wasting time by sniffing at who knows what; I knew next to nothing about what they were doing when they stopped to smell the base of a lamppost or to take a whiff of some secret ambrosia in a neighbour's garden. What I have since learned is that my dogs are up to something tremendously sophisticated. Their sense of smell is thousands of times better than mine, and as they nose around, they are gleaning vast amounts of information about the world around them.

A canine nose has about 300 million receptors, compared with the human nose, which has five or six million. Their noses send signals to the part of the brain that analyzes odours, which is forty times larger than in a human brain. Dogs also have a second sniffing tool called Jacobson's organ, located inside the nasal cavity just above the roof of the mouth, which allows them to detect trace quantities of chemicals around them.

This allows dogs to learn about their environments in exquisite detail. According to a study featured in the journal *Animals*, "Dogs have an extraordinary olfactory capability, which far exceeds that of humans." According to the study, this allows them to "gather both current and historical information about their surrounding environment, but also to find the source of the smell, which is crucial for locating food, danger, or partners for reproduction."

Smelling is their superpower! A dog's sense of smell is so acute that a dog can sniff out odour molecules in the parts per trillion. To put that in perspective, according to one veterinary medicine researcher, dogs can detect the equivalent of a half a teaspoon of sugar in an Olympic-sized swimming pool.

When our body is under stress, it produces odours in our breath and our sweat that is not detectable by humans, but that dogs can smell. If, for instance, we are anxious or frightened, we secrete adrenalin, which is known as the fight-or-flight hormone. Dogs can smell this. A 2022 study from Queen's University Belfast found that, according to lead researcher Clara Wilson, "we, as humans, produce different smells through our sweat and breath when we are stressed, and dogs can tell this apart from our smell when relaxed—even if it is someone they do not know." She also says, "We have lots of evidence that dogs can pick up smells from humans that are associated with certain medical conditions or disease."

While there are other animals that have an equally acute sense of smell, dogs are different because they are temperamentally well suited to human companionship, and they are highly trainable—as you will see in the stories in this book, they are being schooled as service animals that can do remarkable things thanks to their noses. Some breeds are better suited than others for this kind of training. German Shepherds and Golden Retrievers and Labradors are extremely well adapted to become scent detectors—to locate cadavers and sniff out drugs, toxic waste, explosives and illnesses such as cancer, diabetes or infectious disease—in part because their longer snouts have more smell receptors.

Some service dogs are also being trained to detect seizures before they happen, up to forty-five minutes ahead of time in the case of epilepsy, giving the dog time to warn their human to get somewhere safe and avoid serious injury. If a person does seize, the dogs are trained to get their human into a safe position and to get help.

Other service dogs are trained to recognize the scent caused by low blood sugar on a person's breath or through their pores, so they can alert them that they are heading toward hypoglycemia, giving the person time to take the right meds or foods to avoid going into shock. These dogs are so good at their jobs that they can warn of the onset of an episode up to thirty minutes before a blood glucose meter would even register it. A person in a diabetic crisis can present some complicated and confusing behaviours, so these dogs require training to fetch testing materials, glucose tablets, a phone and, if the diabetic person is heading toward shock, another human.

There is another frontier where service dogs are proving useful. Our bodies produce certain chemicals when we are not well, and these are released on our skin and in our sweat, breath and urine. While it is early days yet, there is evidence that some dogs can detect the "odour signatures" of cancers.

The first documented case of a dog detecting cancer was reported in 1989. A two-year-old rescue dog fussed over a mole on his forty-three-year-old owner's back so insistently that she went to her dermatologist, and the mole was subsequently diagnosed as malignant melanoma. Because that dog alerted his owner, she was able to get early treatment for a particularly malicious kind of cancer, and she survived.

Ongoing research is being done into a dog's ability to sniff out breast, colorectal, lung, ovarian and prostate cancer, melanoma, and other types of malignancies. Dogs are also able to detect Parkinson's disease and narcolepsy as well as imminent migraines.

According to work done at the University of California Santa Barbara during the COVID-19 pandemic, professionally trained scent dogs were found to be "as effective and often more effective" at detecting the virus than the rapid antigen tests and PCR tests used in hospitals and testing clinics, even when the patient was asymptomatic.

I used to be woefully ignorant about my dogs' cosmopolitan knowledge of the world, a knowledge informed by each breath they take. But not anymore. Now, every walk we take, I am much more patient about the zig-zaggy route and the sensory feast they are enjoying as we amble around the block. Even when I am in a hurry to get somewhere, I am respectful of the information they are hoovering out of the air, and I'm learning to slow down and pay attention to my own nose, in the hopes of appreciating even a fraction of what my dogs, Calvin and Bowie, are learning about the world.

The canine sense of smell has been studied extensively and is understood quite well, while other behaviours are more of a mystery and something we can only marvel at. In this book you will meet dogs with diverse and impressive abilities: dogs who have an uncanny intelligence that equips them to do heroic things, seemingly out of nowhere; dogs with natural gifts who create unusual roles for themselves; highly trained dogs capable of complex and often life-saving tasks; and dogs who have such huge hearts that they and their owners develop life-giving bonds. And whether an account is of a one-time experience or an ongoing occurrence, each dog in each story in *How My Dog Saved My Life* is a canine guardian angel.

Hero

Ditching Disaster

When Alan chose a name for his Akita puppy, it was as if he were prescient. Six years later, in a remarkable canine rescue, the aptly named "Hero" would save his life.

On the outskirts of small Prairie town, a massive sugar plant sits at the end of a long dirt road. Surrounding it is a scrubby-looking landscape with fields of tall grass. In late March of 2024, Alan and his two dogs, Tora and Hero, went out for a walk in the area; nothing special, just a normal evening wander. While they were walking in the fields, Alan's left leg got hooked on something and he fell forward into a low-lying muddy ditch. The mud went halfway up his shin, and it was like quicksand or wet cement. As Alan tried to pull himself out, the more he struggled, the more his leg became stuck. To make matters worse, he had an injured shoulder from a previous dramatic fall three months earlier, when he had dislocated his shoulder so badly that it took doctors five hours to get it back into place, and he was still recovering from that accident. With only one arm that was useful, he couldn't get enough purchase to pull himself out of the muck.

He was just a few feet from the road when he tripped and fell, but his body was completely obscured from sight by the tall grasses. Temperatures were low enough that patches of snow still dotted the fields, and there was little evening traffic on the dirt road.

Alan is an experienced outdoors person. He grew up on a thousand-acre farm in Manitoba and at age sixty-one is a journeyman structural welder and ironworker, a trade that has taken him to jobs in Alberta and up to the Yukon for six years. He is used to managing the elements. Normally, when Alan ventures out with his dogs, he carries a backpack that's fully kitted out with anything he might need: a knife, water, flashlight, shredded newspaper, lighter and some matches.

That night he anticipated taking just a short walk and he left the pack behind. But fatefully, he forgot his phone. "I'm not one of those people that needs my phone with me 24/7, so I didn't think of it. But when you're stuck there, you think of it. That's a mistake I won't make again!"

Alan's older Akita, Tora, had disappeared into the darkness, but Hero stayed by his side. Alan spent most of that night trying to wrest himself free of the mud, which was like glue around his leg, until he became exhausted with the efforts. Temperatures were heading to below zero, and Alan, fearing he would get chilled, asked his dog for some help. Hero is a big dog, almost one hundred pounds, and has a thick coat, which was useful in this situation. "I got Hero to lie on top of me. He was keeping me warm, and he was licking the mud off my face because at one point I tried—with my forehead and my leg and my arm—to push myself up." Alan had seen a small poplar nearby that might have helped him get some leverage, but the tree was tantalizingly out of reach.

Throughout the rest of that first night, Alan consoled himself by hoping that someone would drive up to the sugar plant in the morning and hear him calling. That was unlikely, though, because it was cold and anyone who drove up the road would have had their car windows closed. When morning broke, no matter how much he yelled, nobody responded. He spent the day lying on his back on the cold ground, with no water and no food. Hero stood sentry, and when the sun began to go down on the second day, Alan knew his situation was progressing from bad to worse. He wasn't so much frightened as he was frustrated. He remembers thinking, "I just don't want to go out this way, I don't want someone to find me dead in a ditch." He pauses, gets a bit choked up and then continues, "And you start thinking about your family, my dogs . . . what's going to happen to them?" Because Alan is such a self-sufficient person—he is single and lives alone—there was no one at home wondering why he had gone missing.

As the sun set that evening, he again began shouting for help. Whenever he raised his voice, the coyotes would howl, and that had an impact on him. "Probably the only time I was really, I wouldn't use the word frightened, but worried, is when the coyotes would howl. Every time I hollered, they were thinking, 'Oh, an easy meal.' I'm used to hearing coyotes howl, but what made it worse is that I knew they were close," he says. He heard rustling in the bushes nearby, and assumed it was the coyotes. That was confirmed when, around midnight, Hero took off. "Five minutes or so later, I heard the coyotes yelping. Ten minutes after that Hero was back," he says, with pride. "They were close enough that when Hero got after them, I could hear them yelp."

Alan didn't hear another sound from the coyotes that night, but he was far from safe. It was frigidly cold (–7°C) and his body temperature was falling precipitously. "I knew my time was short. I was shaking so bad I was vibrating," he says. Alan was more and more at risk of succumbing to hypothermia, but over and above that, he was frustrated. "I've never been in a situation I can't control, but this was a situation I couldn't control or get myself out of. I needed to rely on Hero to do that for me. I called him over and said to him, 'Hero, you have to go and get Daddy help. If you don't, Daddy is going to be dead in the morning.' And he was gone."

It is impressive that Hero was so attuned to Alan's perilous situation. In part it was because Akitas were bred to be fierce and courageous protectors. The breed originates from the mountains of northern Japan, where they were used for hunting and as guard dogs, and they develop an intensely strong bond with their owners.

In Japan, when a child is born, the parents are given a small statue of an Akita—as a symbol of protection and health, happiness and long life. For all their admirable qualities, Akitas are strong and territorial; this makes them the right dog for only certain situations and owners.

Alan's dogs are well trained, but they are house pets, not support animals. Still, Hero somehow understood that his owner needed him to go and get assistance, and he ran toward town, about 2.5 kilometres away. Hero showing up in town unattended was something people noted. He is a large dog who has an imperial look to him, with a luxuriant double coat of white hair, a brown and black face, and very dark ears that stand straight up on his head. "I walk a lot with the dogs and people noticed that he was by himself, so somebody mentioned that there was something wrong," Alan says.

Very early that morning local police had received a call about Hero running loose, but they were unable to track him down. Later, Hero got into a scuffle with another dog that was walking off leash. The owner of that dog managed to separate them, but he and the dogs were injured in the process. He contacted the police, who went looking for Hero again. Hero had returned to be with Alan. "He knew I was in trouble," says Alan, whose first thought when he saw the dog again was, "I'm not going to die."

The police finally spotted Hero lying on a berm beside the road, just a few feet from where Alan lay hidden in the grasses. When the police car pulled up toward the dog, Alan's calls for help caught the attention of the officer, who had his window rolled down. The officer whistled, heard another loud shriek for help, and Alan remembers the moment he heard the officer say, "I can hear you. Where are you?" Alan replied, "Just keep following my voice."

When he heard the officer say that he could see him, Alan remembers thinking, "I was finally found." The relief still palpable in his voice, Alan says, "My dog saved my life. He did what I asked him to."

The police got to work quickly. They called an ambulance, which arrived not long after, as did an animal bylaw enforcement officer. There was one inadvertently amusing exchange when the officer asked Alan what his dog's name was. "I said, 'Hero.'" Alan laughs, remembering that the officer replied, "Yes, I know he's a hero. What's his name?" This banter went back and forth until Alan clarified, "His name is H-E-R-O. His name really is Hero."

It took a great deal of effort to pull Alan out of the mud. He had to be immobilized on a backboard to get him out of the ditch without hurting him further. "They rolled me over to get the backboard underneath me, and because the mud was so thick, it sucked the backboard in, and it took four of them to actually break the backboard loose with me on it to get me into the ambulance."

Alan's core temperature was at a dangerously low 30 degrees Celsius. If a person's core temperature falls below 35 degrees Celsius, it is considered a medical emergency, and heart and respiratory systems can fail. Paramedics wrapped Alan in blankets and gave him a shot of dextrose to get his blood sugar levels back up quickly, since he'd had nothing to eat or drink for two days. While they were stabilizing Alan, Hero sat nearby, vigilant. The Akita became quite agitated about the people milling about Alan and began growling at them, but the familiar, soothing voice of his owner calmed him, and once Alan was safely in the ambulance, Hero settled down. "The officer told me later, 'That dog was going to protect you right to the bitter end. If you weren't conscious, we never would have got close to you, if you didn't calm him down,'" Alan says.

Alan and Hero's concern for each other was mutual. Alan had reason to worry. Hero also needed some medical attention—the dog had sustained injuries in his encounter with the coyotes, and being out in the cold for two days, without food or water, wasn't good for a dog any more than it was for a human. "They took him to the vet to get him patched up because he was a little cut up from fighting with the coyotes," Alan says. "One of the bylaw officers said, 'He's bleeding. He's going to need some stitches.'" Fortunately, the vet was able to glue Hero's cuts together instead of having to use stitches, and Hero was then taken into care by Lost Paws, a local rescue organization, until he could be reunited with Alan. Meanwhile, Alan's second dog, fifteen-year-old Tora, was found hiding in the backyard of Alan's home, hungry and cold but otherwise all right, and Lost Paws took her into their shelter too.

Alan was admitted to a local hospital for nine days. His doctors were worried he might need to go on dialysis because he had become dehydrated. Lying on his back in the cold could also have done some serious damage to his kidneys. Luckily, once they had flushed him with fluids and got some antibiotics into him, he recovered. "I'm fully healed again, back to where I was before the accident," Alan says.

When Alan was released from hospital, he had an emotional reunion with his dogs. "It was probably the happiest day of my life," Alan says. He took the dogs to the police station to meet everyone and thank them for what they had done for him. Lost Paws had set up a GoFundMe campaign, which raised close to $3,000 in forty-eight hours to cover all his vet bills. He still gets choked up when he talks about how members of the Tabor community stepped up to help. Alan is a loner and has spent most of his adult life in the company of his dogs, and when he learned about how the community responded to his accident, Alan says, "I felt a surge of gratefulness for everything people around me did: the medical staff in the hospital, the people of Tabor, Lost Paws. How do you say thank you and repay everything everybody did?" His way of paying forward his gratitude is to buy food for dogs with special dietary needs and donate it to the shelter.

Alan will probably be reflecting on his two dark nights in the cold for a long time. And he'll most likely mull over some fundamental questions he came face-to-face with while lying in that ditch, wondering if he'd get out of there alive. "I'm not hugely religious, but it makes you think, 'Why am I still here?'" And, he says, it has also led him to wonder, "Where do I go from here?"

Not many of us have stood so close to the brink of death, but in the wake of his harrowing experience, Alan is very mindful about how fortunate he was to have his fierce protector by his side. And fortunately, he will have many more chances to muse on these big life questions, every time he and Hero hit the trails.

Stinky

Rescuer Rescued

George is one of the most sophisticated and innovative canine trainers in Canada. There have been many remarkable dogs in his life, and more than a few have rescued him from precarious situations. But there is one above all the others that saved his life—a Rottweiler named Stinky.

When George first adopted her as a puppy, she was just Nikki. She was given the nickname Stinky after a run-in with two skunks. She was a big dog, with a black and tan coat. She had a broad head and the tan markings around her muzzle made it look like she was smiling.

George was born in Winnipeg in 1958, into a large and very close family. George's mother is German, his father is Cree. As a youngster, he didn't really know he was Indigenous. "When we were growing up, we didn't talk about it a lot because it really wasn't a good thing to be an Indian," he says. It wasn't something the family hid; they just didn't discuss it. Looking back, though, he remembers that his father, in fact all of his family, were hassled because they were Indigenous.

George is a plain-spoken, boisterous man with a big laugh, broad smile and warm eyes. He is a true innovator, generous beyond the call of duty, and has invited strangers in need to crash at his house—sometimes for months.

A social justice maverick, George has been working with organizations in the Aboriginal community for his entire professional life. He is a First Nations band constable, and he founded, in concert with Aboriginal Elders and First Nations leadership, an organization called Meghan Search and Rescue (MSAR) to help address the issue of missing and murdered Aboriginal people in Manitoba, at a time when no attention was being paid to them at all.

As a search commander for MSAR, George has been on hundreds of search and rescue missions, gruelling work that could have destroyed others with a less enduring spirit. But over time, even George found the cumulative impact of what he witnessed had an injurious effect on him. "You're under the expectation that you're looking for someone and they're going to be alive. You're working in remote Aboriginal communities and generally it's already too late. You're looking with the best intention, and then you find the dead body," he says, choking up. He has written about the horrific things he witnessed. "I have seen people dead in all forms—frozen, burnt, drowned, dead for minutes, days, weeks, months, mutilated, ravaged by wildlife." The discovery of a body was tough enough, but George was also horrified by the cruel things people had done to each other. The impact on the families hoping a loved one could be found alive was also difficult to witness. "There's this huge wall of grief that happens, screaming and crying, and it chills you," he says. "After a while you go into a dark hole." George paid a personal price for doing this painful, traumatic work, but he knew it was absolutely necessary and powerfully rewarding.

As a Certified Master Dog Trainer, George developed an MSAR-sponsored program to train hundreds of working dogs for first responders—the police, search and rescue personnel, and the military. (A burgeoning number of George's training programs take place around the world, and MSAR has placed more than six thousand service dogs globally.)

He also trains service dogs for persons with disabilities. Over the years, he began to sense that personal support dogs could be uniquely helpful to military veterans and first responders. At the time, post-traumatic stress disorder was poorly understood; in the early 2000s, there were next to no programs to help people cope with the fallout from the horrific things they had witnessed in combat and conflict situations. "We were doing a lot of critical intervention with guys so they wouldn't kill themselves," he explains, "because the guys were killing themselves every day."

Which is how Stinky came into George's life. When he adopted her as a puppy, back in 2000, he wanted to train her for the special program he was creating for people with PTSD. When she finished her training, Stinky was the first dog to graduate from MSAR's Elite Psychiatric Therapy Dog Program and she became one of the first service dogs in Canada to work with people suffering from post-traumatic stress disorder. For his part, George became the first Canadian first responder to have a PTSD service dog.

Among her many skills, Stinky was taught to sense physiological changes in the body, like increasing heart rate that is brought on when a person is agitated or anxious; she was trained to distract her owner long enough for symptoms to subside, helping them stave off aggressive or violent behaviour. If a person needed psychological support, she was trained to stick close to them for as long as they needed. If they became unsettled or frightened in a crowd, Stinky managed crowd anxiety by creating space around the person. And if a person was having nightmares, she would wake them and apply deep pressure therapy (DPT) if they needed it, until their central nervous system calmed down. Stinky's calm presence helped with depression, providing the emotional support and structure people needed to get out of bed and leave their homes. In short, she was trained to give them back their lives.

It was ironic that the dog George trained to save other people's lives ended up saving his. As it turns out, George had his own first-hand knowledge of the need for a service animal. He says he had "complex PTSD," brought on by trauma—from his childhood and from his job. Stinky helped him manage the symptoms when he was tormented by flashbacks, nightmares, depression or outbursts of anger. "What I noticed is I got a lot less violent. I wasn't getting into fights in Walmart. I wasn't punching people out at gas stations," he says. "The general public doesn't understand, when you come across somebody with PTSD and you agitate them, the switch goes. That's a whole other level of aggression than you've ever seen."

George has written about his experience, saying he withdrew into himself, becoming isolated and avoiding the outside world. He would go months where he wasn't sleeping well or eating properly, doing all the wrong things to try to numb how he was feeling. Medications didn't work for him, "but what did was having dogs," he writes. "When I wake from a nightmare, sweating and screaming, I see two paws on my chest and a little happy face licking me and trying to calm me down—bringing me back from the darkness, bringing me back to the now."

There were times when George found it difficult to de-escalate his own emotions because of conflict situations he dealt with during a shift as a band constable. "I'd go out in public—I was still agitated and I was still aggressive," he says. Stinky was a calm presence who helped him control his volatile behaviour. "I'll go for a walk, or I'll take my dog with me and hang out. And what it does is it grounds me." When he was agitated, Stinky would provide DPT to calm his nervous system. She was a calming presence, and slowly, his life began to take on a better shape.

But there was one jarring year, not long after George got Stinky, when George's life was upended by a laundry list of calamities. "I think it was 2001 or 2002, two of my best friends died, my grandmother died, my wife and I separated, I got sick, I lost my business, I lost my house. You name it," he says, remembering that his brother once said to him, "I can't believe you didn't blow your head off . . . that was crazy." If not for Stinky, this was the year he might not have survived.

While Stinky was the first dog to save George's life, life had a way of repeatedly putting him in harm's way and there were other dogs that kept him alive over the years. There was Benny: Some years ago, George was in a serious car accident that has left him suffering seizures. One day, his dog Benny, an Australian Shepherd trained to anticipate changes to George's behaviour fifteen to twenty minutes ahead of the onset of a seizure, kept him from making a potentially disastrous mistake. George wanted to run some errands, but Benny wouldn't get in the car. George cajoled him to jump into the vehicle, but the dog was immoveable. George relented and they went back into the house. Five minutes later, George had a seizure. "Thank God I wasn't driving, because I would have been on the highway. That would have been bad news," he says.

And there was Maggie. Once, while out in the bush on a rescue, George and his crew were chased by a black bear. "This bear's coming at us full tilt, the guy in front of us with the shotgun drops the gun and runs. And I'm helping another guy that got injured," he says. "I had my police dog, Maggie. She runs at it full tilt and I'm like, 'Oh shit, there goes my dog.'" Maggie did what George describes as "pulling a Husky," running right underneath the bear. "And as the bear was turned around, she bit him in the ass, bit him in the leg, and then she just stood her ground," he remembers, still amazed. "And the bear took off!" In an altercation with a bear, says George, it's: "Brown bear, lie down. Black bear, say your prayers." Luckily Maggie was unfamiliar with this mantra.

And there was Tony. In another near miss, one winter George was riding a quad on a frozen lake, with his dog Tony in a skid behind him. "This guy came blowing past me in a Ski-Doo," he remembers. "Then he just disappeared. He fell through the ice. I'm like, 'Oh, shit.' I go racing over there, and I throw the [rescue] bag. He doesn't get it. I throw the bag again; he doesn't get it. So I get on my stomach and I start crawling over." George is experienced in ice rescues, but "Tony is freaking out, barking because he doesn't want me to go there." The dog ran circles around George, jumping around and insisting that he bring the man out onto the ice from another spot. George did get the man out safely and only realized later that the ice was too thin where he had initially been heading. Tony saved not one but two men that day.

George has another memory that he shares somewhat sheepishly. "I've got to tell you about the time I got humbled by a dog. I'd just come off this huge search and my head's like, this big;

I think I'm Jesus, right?" When George got called out for another search, he agreed to go, ill-prepared. About six miles into the search, George discovered that he'd done something foolish. He'd become separated from the other members of the search party, and he hadn't checked his gear. His radio, his SAT phone and his emergency beacon were all dead. And he was completely lost. "I'm standing there and I'm like, 'You idiot,'" George says. Tony had continued ahead, tracking the person they'd been looking for, and luckily, when he'd successfully completed that task, he found the search team and brought them to George. It was a source of much relief, and much mirth, among the team members. "They're like, 'Hey, superstar, we found you with your own dog,'" George says, laughing. "I got bugged about that for, oh God, years."

To this day, George is never without a dog and, in fact, is usually surrounded by many. One friend describes being at George's house once while there were twenty police dogs in his living room, all lying down, perfectly well behaved. Although George has learned to manage his PTSD, it doesn't go away and nighttime can, at times, still be challenging. He takes comfort in the vigilance of the three or four German Shepherds who now sleep in his room. They are just the latest in a long string of canine companions, starting with Stinky, that all have one essential thing in common: they rescued the rescuer.*

---

* As I was doing some final tinkering with the book before it went to press, I learned that George had died suddenly, just shy of his fifty-ninth birthday. As I understand it, he sat down for a nap and didn't wake up. It was a total shock. George was a comet; he lived large, and his death leaves a huge hole in the dog-training universe.

Marcy

Mini Marvel

From as far back as he can remember, Lucas wished—knew—he was a boy. It never felt quite right to him that he had been born in a female body, and that infiltrated every part of his consciousness. "I had this fear of playing with other children because they were like, 'You're a girl,' so they would treat me like a girl. I became this really, really introverted child who spent a lot of time by myself."

In a world where he felt out of sync, the one thing he was never uncertain about was the kinship he felt with dogs—they have been unfailing amigos and allies. His first experience of this was with a Beagle, his beloved childhood pet. "I would say that my dog was my best friend and confidant . . . that connection was always something that felt really safe to me because he didn't care what gender I was. He was just, 'You're my pal,'" he remembers.

Four decades later, a fifteen-pound canine miracle would come into Lucas's life—but before he got to her, he had to face some formidable challenges.

Lucas's sense that his body didn't align with his identity caused him much confusion and grief. In his early twenties he came out as a lesbian and lived this way for years, but still didn't feel right. Trying to anaesthetize his gender dysphoria, he was drinking heavily and doing a lot of drugs, which were just making a mess of his life. Transitioning to a man seemed like an impossibility to him in the early 1990s. Lucas says, "I thought I was mentally ill, and I thought I had to fix it, because how could that be real? How could I be a different gender?"

Lucas became a musician, the lead singer in a rock band; by the time he was twenty-one, his music career was beginning to take off. He was driven and passionate about his music, but he worried that "nobody wanted to see a bull-dyke onstage playing guitar" and that audiences wouldn't respond to him unless he looked like a more traditional female rocker. He forced himself into an extreme femininity, but the misalignment of what he was projecting onstage versus what he was feeling inside sent him into a downward spiral that eventually led to a complete nervous breakdown. "Something in my brain just could not manage this identity anymore. I didn't really know it at the time, but I went into a dissociative state or a state of psychosis," he says. "I had to stay home for three years. I had agoraphobia, and I couldn't go outside. It was a mess." His parents, who were always very supportive, postponed a move back to Portugal and he moved in with them.

When he was twenty-four, he stumbled into dog walking as a business, which he did for eight years. He was never happier than when he was with his "pack." "It was such a good job," he remembers; "working outside with animals, for me, that's the life!" While being with the dogs felt great, the rest of his life still seemed out of whack. He came out as trans when he was thirty-two, and had top surgery the next year. The day they removed his bandages he remembers looking down and bawling his eyes out. "It was one of the happiest moments of my life," he says. "I just felt like, oh my God, I'm coming home." The joy was somewhat short-lived because, although he was living as a man, he couldn't complete his transition by taking testosterone for fear of losing his singing voice. "Having top surgery was the only thing that I could do to masculinize my body at that stage, and that was incredibly disappointing and depressing."

Meanwhile, he became the first openly trans man to be signed to a record label, and he and his band were enjoying big success and were on the road all the time. He had to give up his dog-walking business—the hardest job he ever had to quit, he says.

During these years, he was able to take the testosterone he needed to complete his transition, and he found love, got married and had a domestic life. But there were casualties. He describes himself as a functioning alcoholic, but when he was forty-three his marriage broke up and he lost his two dogs in a custody battle with his wife. It was devasting, one of the greatest heartbreaks of his life.

Lucas began to descend further and further into a quagmire of mental health problems. The combination of the wrong medications and recreational drugs and alcohol took him to some very dark places. "I caught myself having really intense suicidal thoughts," he says. "I called it 'the grocery list of suicide,' and I'd be like, 'I'm going to go buy a pack of cigarettes, I'm going to have a sandwich, and then I'm going to kill myself.'" He took himself off the prescription meds, but he still wasn't okay. "I kept drinking and drinking and drinking and smoking weed and taking acid and mushrooms, and I got lost in that world for a very long time. I also got lost in anger," he remembers. The people in Lucas's life had no idea what was going on with him, and he says they assumed his bad behaviour was because he was just being an asshole.

And then Marcy, a fifteen-pound miracle, came into his life. "It's so funny how it always comes back to the dogs," he says. "I am not a person who does life without a dog. I just am not."

Lucas decided that he wanted a Chihuahua. "I started putting that out in the universe. And this very strange thing happened." One day, in a park in west end Toronto, Lucas ran into a woman he knew, and with her she had a sweet little black and brown Chihuahua puppy named Marcy. Lucas was instantly smitten with the dog—she was so tiny, swimming in a sweater that was way too big for her. She has a two-toned brown and tan coat, with endearingly ginormous ears and a very long pink tongue. Shortly after that encounter, his phone rang, and it was the same woman. "She left this frantic message," he says. "It was, 'Please take my dog. I don't want to give her to anybody else but you. I know she's supposed to be yours.'" When he called her back, she explained that she was now a single mum and couldn't take care of the dog anymore. Lucas told her he lived in a situation where he couldn't have a dog that barked, and she swore that this dog never barked. "I thought she was completely and utterly lying to me, because there is no such thing as a non-barking Chihuahua," he says, but he couldn't resist and agreed to take Marcy on a trial basis. As soon as she got in his car, he thought, "This is going to be a foster fail galore!" Miraculously, the woman hadn't been lying; months passed without a peep from Marcy. The first time Lucas heard her bark was after he left her with a friend whose dog barked whenever someone came to the door. "And when she came back," he says, laughing, "Marcy barked for the first time and it scared the bejesus out of me."

Marcy had arrived at just the right time. Lucas was still drinking, but having Marcy helped him put on the brakes—a bit. He couldn't drink until all hours and sleep in every morning because he had to get up to let Marcy out to do her business. "I had to be sober during the day because there's no way I'm going to be walking my dog around the streets of Toronto while I'm hammered. So my rules were: You drink at night, but Marcy needs to be safe, so you wake up in the morning; you walk her midday, and then at night; after she's gone to bed, after her ten o'clock walk, you can drink. And so, I did."

And then COVID happened. Lucas's world became further unstitched, and he is very clear that without Marcy he wouldn't have made it through. He had slowed down his drinking, but his mental health issues were being stoked by the pandemic. "I think I would have drowned in my paranoid thoughts. I think I would have drowned in alcohol. I had started destroying all my friendships because of the paranoia," he says. "I had so much time on my hands, and along with alcohol, that started fuelling hallucinations and it just got horrible."

It was Marcy, and her needs, that kept him from completely losing it. "She was the one who got me up in the morning. She was the one who made sure that I took care of myself enough that I never put her in danger. She was almost like my little guide; she was leading me without me even realizing what was happening. I just thought, 'Oh, I'm being responsible.'" That seemed to be enough, until he came to from a blackout and found himself sitting on his couch with no idea what had happened. Marcy was beside him, and he realized he was seriously in crisis. She was fine, but he was terrified that he could have done something to hurt her, and so, to ensure he didn't put her in harm's way again, he found someone to care for her and checked himself into a local mental health hospital. When he finally got a diagnosis of late-onset schizoaffective disorder, whose symptoms include depression, hallucinations and delusions, things began to make sense. With appropriate treatment and the right medications, he began to inch back toward some stability. And he got sober.

Lucas and Marcy were reunited, and he has begun to walk dogs again. He loves it, and he often brings Marcy along with him. Things are up and down, but in a much more manageable way than before. "The struggles that I have these days come and go, depending on the way life is going. I'll struggle with agoraphobia sometimes, and that is where Marcy comes in. When I told my psychiatrist she said, 'Why don't we just make her your therapy dog?'" She wrote him a note to that effect, and he got Marcy a little vest so he can take her everywhere.

Marcy may not be a trained support animal, but because she is so loved and she reciprocates, the bond has been tremendously healing to Lucas. "She saved my life in ways that are so interesting . . . When I have a dog, it feels like a bond with a beautiful, precious, forever child. I think I have to love, protect and give this beautiful, helpless little creature the most protection and happiness that they are going to have in this short life. And the thing is, they do the same for you without even trying.

"Dogs are innately love," he says, adding, "I've made a complete recovery. I never thought I'd ever be in this place in my life, ever!"

Rory Michael

Guardian's Guardian

Katherine (Kitti) is the embodiment of the Good Samaritan. As a human rights activist, she has found herself in the middle of civil wars in Central America, at the heart of natural disasters all over the world, and at Ground Zero in the aftermath of the 9/11 terrorist bombings. She has witnessed, and been the victim of, horrendous torture and sexual abuse, all of which have scarred her emotionally, left her with profound PTSD and taken a terrible toll on her body. And if it weren't for a remarkable Standard Poodle named Rory Michael, who watches over her day and night, Kitti would have been close to death many times over.

Kitti became acquainted with grief much too early. When she was twelve years old, her mother died of cancer, and memories of her mother's suffering and her kindness still bring Kitti to tears. "If there was anybody that I could grow up to be as good as, it would be my mom—that kind of heart and that kind of soul. She was my inspiration." Her mother's example pointed Kitti toward a life of empathy. "Having lost my mother, I understood what horrific grief was. And as far as I was concerned, I felt there was no pain like it."

Now an engaged and engaging woman in her mid-sixties, Kitti is a fighter despite what she has seen and experienced. A lifelong Albertan, she was born in Calgary and now lives in Drumheller, a town northeast of Calgary that is famous for its dinosaur fossils.

As a young woman in the 1980s, Kitti worked with an organization called Change the Children, which ran projects for the poorest of the poor in Central America. Her trips to some of these projects fuelled her commitment to social justice, but one such visit had a catastrophic impact on her life. "I was down in El Salvador during the civil war in 1986. A friend of mine and I were captured and held in what is called the Treasury, which is where seventy thousand people were tortured and disappeared. We were tortured for eight days and released."

When Kitti says they were "released," she means she and her colleague were thrown into a dump by the death squads and left for dead. They had been hideously abused. "I was stabbed multiple times in the chest. They pulled out eight teeth," Kitti remembers. "They didn't want to waste bullets, so they would put syringes in your arm full of battery acid and they would talk about pushing that in. Then they would bring other people into the cell and put battery acid in them so you would see what happened."

Miraculously she and her colleague lived, although they were gravely injured. Kitti managed to crawl to a nearby house to ask for help, and thanks to a sympathetic local veterinarian who patched them up, they got out of the country safely.

Despite the brutality of her experience, Kitti wasn't dissuaded from pursuing her activism. "I learned about man's inhumanity to man, how horrific it can be. And I remember vowing to myself that I would do whatever it took to try and help other people that were marginalized, that were disadvantaged, that were affected by war, by poverty, by cruelty." Back on home turf, Kitti turned her head to studying numerous disciplines, including world religions. "I figured it was very important to understand different cultures and different political systems," she says. "I studied psychology for trauma, and then I did my residency as a psychiatric chaplain at the Rocky View Hospital." At that hospital Kitti met a doctor who specialized in PTSD, and she began helping people struggling with PTSD, which dovetailed well with her training as a secular chaplain when she went where needed, to war zones and to help in the wake of natural disasters—mudslides and earthquakes.

She was carrying her own heavy psychosocial burden, something called "sanctuary trauma." It is a particularly complicated form of PTSD that makes a person feel unsafe with persons in authority. "Where you would normally go for help to somebody in uniform—a priest, a medic, a doctor—they're the ones that hurt you. There's always a doctor present when you're being tortured, because if you're unconscious, you can't give them any information. If you're dead, you can't give them any information," she says. "To this day, I'm terrified of male doctors, really afraid of people in uniform."

Thirty some years after her experience in El Salvador, Kitti responded to a new call for help. When planes flew into the World Trade Center and the city of New York asked for help, she headed straight to Ground Zero. "I would work in the pit one day digging out body parts, and then work with the firefighters and do grief counselling, trauma counselling and support." Kitti remembers it as a highly charged emotional experience. Because she is an interfaith chaplain, she was enlisted to accompany body parts to the morgue. "On the way to the morgue, just before you got there, pretty much every police officer, every firefighter, every first responder was lined up to salute that ambulance coming by, knowing that it was a fallen comrade. And every single time it brought me to tears. Every single time."

First responders were not equipped with the proper gear for the job, Kitti says; they only had little blue paper masks for protection. She had no idea that, day after day for three weeks, she was breathing air poisoned with toxins from four hundred tons of crushed concrete, glass and asbestos. "More of us have died now because of lung problems and diseases attributed to exposure than died in the Twin Towers themselves." Nor did she understand that the myriad toxic chemicals she was exposed to, heavy metals like antimony, would wreak such havoc on her health. The personal fallout from her three weeks working at the 9/11 site is that she now has a particularly dangerous form of asthma. It's known as "silent asthma" because it doesn't display any of the usual asthma symptoms like wheezing or coughing. "I don't make any noise when my oxygen levels go down," she explains. "I don't turn blue."

Just as silently and injuriously, the cumulative impact of repeated trauma crept up on her. Somewhat ironically, the tipping point was an event that happened in a Canadian hospital. Kitti describes being "retraumatized" during a visit to the emergency ward. "I wasn't breathing well at all," she remembers. "I went into Emergency a lot. The doctors are fantastic, they're wonderful humanitarians, but this one, sadly, was not. It was all about control. I said, 'I'm very fearful around male doctors. The psychologists have asked that I have Ativan to calm down a bit.' He said, 'Would you like fries with that? You think you can come in here and order what you want?' I said, 'May I see a female physician?' He said again, 'Do you want fries with that? You cannot come in here and order this or this or this.' Fortunately, I had one of my best friends with me, who happened to be a nurse, and she said, 'Kitti, we're getting out of here.'" Her friend wanted to take her to a nearby big city hospital, but, Kitti says, "Once he heard that, he said, 'You're not leaving.' And I said, 'Yeah, I am.' And he goes, 'No, no, you're too sick to leave. We don't know what's causing the lack of oxygen.' I said, 'Well, right now it's fear. When I have a horrific fear response, my oxygen levels go way, way down to the point that I go into respiratory arrest. And that's very serious. I need to get away from you because I'm so afraid of you.' So he called security and had security come tie me up to the bed." Kitti was so frightened, her oxygen levels took a nosedive and hospital staff had to call a code.

Kitti decided she had to do something to cope. She approached Spirasi, a highly specialized national centre for victims of torture in Dublin, Ireland. "They took my case. They investigated it. The head of Spirasi is Rory Halpin. He'd also been a Jesuit priest in a previous life and many of his friends were Jesuit priests that were tortured and assassinated in El Salvador. So he knew the situation. I flew to Dublin, and I was there for two months under intensive treatment."

Spirasi helped Kitti deal with PTSD and OSI (the term "operational stress injury" refers to extreme psychological stress experienced by first responders) as well as the trauma caused by the incident with the doctor in the hospital. It was the Spirasi staff who steered her toward getting a dog. Kitti says they were adamant about it, telling her, "We don't want you going back to

Canada unless you have a service dog that can alert you to the phenomenal drop in oxygen that can result in complete respiratory arrest and then cardiac arrest."

Kitti began looking for a service dog even before she left Ireland. She found a breeder near Lethbridge, Alberta, who had an eight-week-old black Standard Poodle puppy. The day after she landed home from Dublin, she picked him up.

She named the pup Rory Michael—Rory after Rory Halpin, and Michael after Saint Michael the Archangel. She set about training him straightaway. She undertook obedience training, but her dog was going to require more than basic skills.

Rory Michael is long-legged and slim with grey-black curly hair. He has an ever-curious expression and, depending on which haircut he's sporting, he has a long slender schnozzle or a fuzzy face with an expression that looks eager to say hello.

Kitti had been told by numerous dog-training schools that her needs were too complex for their dogs. After much searching, however, she did find the right school, a non-profit organization called Courageous Companions that trains and certifies Elite K-9 Service dogs for military veterans and first responders. They agreed that, if she wanted to train her own dog, they would help her and get him certified.

Rory Michael underwent comprehensive training, including learning to do a kind of canine CPR. He has his own "business card," given to him by Courageous Companions, which says: "Hi, my name is Rory Michael. I've undergone specialized training to provide life-saving assistance to my handler. Some of the tasks I perform are emergency breathing alerts, cardiac alerts and medication retrieval. I was born on September 11th, which is very special as my handler was a first responder at the 9/11 site in New York City."

Kitti and her dog are so in sync that he responds when she has an asthma attack. Kitti says, "Rory Michael saves my life, absolutely saves my life when that happens. He can smell cortisol building up in my system." Cortisol is the stress hormone humans release when they are under acute psychological and/or physiological stress, and it can be detected through changes in their breath and their sweat. Because dogs have a sense of smell that is so much more acute than that of humans, they sense changes in human breath and sweat with almost 95 percent accuracy. Dogs like Rory Michael are trained how to react and how to protect their owner.

When Kitti is at risk, Rory Michael comes over to her, places his paws on her shoulders, puts his face up close to hers, and touches her face repeatedly with his nose. He does this at the pace of measured breathing, and if she's panicked, she follows along with him, which is calming. "Right now he's snoring, hanging out on the couch behind me. But if I need him, he's right here, right now. We are that much in sync, that attuned," she says.

When Kitti is dealing with an emotional issue, she might begin to shake or, rarely, cry. When Rory Michael notices, she says, "he will come running across the room" to rescue her. "And now all I have to do is go like this"—she puts her face in her hands, as though crying—"and he comes," Kitti says. "There has to be that phenomenal connection. I am absolutely blessed that I have Rory Michael because he's completely in tune with me."

Rory Michael carries a little first aid kit around his neck. It's a neon green pouch attached to his collar that contains a pulse oximeter to measure Kitti's oxygen levels, and medicines that will buy her time to get on the phone and call for help. There have been times when Rory Michael sensed trouble way ahead of his owner. "He'll stare me in the eyes like, 'Do I have to write it out for you, woman? Would you take your pulse oximeter out and see what your oxygen levels are?' So I do. If I ignore him, he'll then put his paws up on my shoulder and stare me right in the eyes, like, 'You're not listening to me!'" One day Kitti was watching TV, completely unaware that anything was wrong. Her oxygen levels, which should normally be at around 95 percent saturation, had dropped down to 64. "Had he not done anything, I'd have gone to bed, and I would have died that night. So he saved my life that time."

Going into distress is a matter of life and death for Kitti. Normally, service dogs are trained to do what their handlers tell them, but it was crucial that she train him to overrule her in certain circumstances. "We have to teach them how to break a command, how to be disobedient to save your life. And that's one of the hardest things to do with a dog because they think, 'Well, I have to listen to her.' For them to know that saving your life is more important than the command it overrides is phenomenal." This happened one day during an outing to the Drumheller Dinosaur Museum. "We sat down for a little break and Rory came up and put his paws up on me and I was like, 'I'm fine. Go sit down!'" Rory Michael persisted until Kitti relented. "I put my finger in the pulse oximeter. It was in the low seventies. My friend Chris put me in his car and took me to hospital, which is half an hour away. I was completely unconscious by the time I got there; my oxygen was so low. Out in public, I didn't have a clue my O_2 levels were silently going down, but Rory Michael wouldn't leave me alone."

When Kitti came home from Dublin, Spirasi had given her a medic alert card that she keeps with her. It says, "I am a survivor of torture. I panic in medical situations. It is important that I perceive a sense of control. Please ask my permission before attempting aid. Please use female physicians when possible. Thank you for your cooperation."

Rory Michael gives Kitti confidence that if she's in trouble he will be there for her, and having him by her side gives her the freedom to be out in the world. If Kitti is unwell, she tends to "turtle," she says. "If I get sick, if I get afraid, I don't go out. I don't contact my friends. I become completely introverted. He allows me to get out. He allows me to even go to medical appointments, which I avoided like the plague before, even something like going out to get blood tests or whatever. I couldn't do it. I had what's called a graveyard of medical requisitions. I was too afraid to go out and do it. Now I can go do that." And because she feels safe, she can leave her home and volunteer in her community. She's done work with the Red Cross, and she still presides, with Rory Michael by her side, over funerals for those who can't afford them.

She has found joy too. She's volunteered with the Girl Guides of Canada, where, as a leader with the youngest girls, who are called Brownies, she and Rory Michael were given special names. "The leaders are Owls. They called me Star Owl and they named him Wolf Owl. He responds to that. He goes round and round in the fairy ring. He dances with the girls. They wanted to make him into a princess. They decorate his hair for Christmas. He is so gentle, they just love him."

Clover

Dramatic Devotion

What began as an unremarkable daily ritual abruptly morphed into a remarkable—and alarming—event for Haley and the family dog, Clover.

Every morning, regular as clockwork, twenty-eight-year-old Haley and two-year-old Clover walked around the block in their suburban neighbourhood, a routine that has been in place ever since Clover came into the family as a puppy. That day in March 2020 began no differently. As they were making their way along a quiet street about five minutes from home, Haley's knees buckled and she collapsed onto a snowbank beside the road, completely losing consciousness. Clover rushed over to Haley and tried to rouse her by nudging her head and body. Surprisingly, a car drove right by while Haley was lying in a heap on the ground, visibly convulsing from the seizure. She would have been hard to miss, especially with an eighty-pound

Maremma Sheepdog mix, with a luminous white coat, standing beside her on the pavement.

After the car passed, Clover became increasingly agitated. When Haley didn't respond, she began jumping up and down frantically, pulling on her leash until she freed herself from Haley's grasp. In doing so, she caused Haley to roll onto her side. "I think it's miraculous that whatever she was trying to do, making Haley roll over was huge, because she literally was in the mud and snow and slush," Haley's mother, Diane, says, adding how frightening it was to consider what could have happened if she had remained face down.

When Clover saw a van coming around a bend in the road, she sprang into the middle of the street and stood in front of the vehicle, refusing to move. The twenty-one-year-old driver of the van stopped, leapt out and, seeing Haley, ran to her side. He then ran to the nearest door, rang the doorbell again and again to try to get help, ran back to Haley, and stayed with her until an ambulance arrived. All Haley remembers is regaining consciousness in the ambulance, completely confused and deeply frightened.

During all this, Clover stood a short distance away, keeping a watchful eye on Haley. Neighbours came out to see what the commotion was, and when any of them tried to approach the dog, she kept her distance. Once emergency help arrived, it was almost as if Clover knew that she then needed to alert her family. She made a beeline for home, solo, avoiding a potentially dangerous busy street on the way. Haley's father, Randall, and her sister, Riley, answered the door to Clover, who was frantically barking, and a neighbour who had come to alert them. When they saw the dog, but no Haley, they knew something was awry and raced to where paramedics were still doing triage with Haley. When they got to her, Randall says that it was terrifying to see his daughter incoherent in the ambulance, with a face full of mud.

Haley's seizure and the aftermath were caught on a security camera that a neighbour had trained onto the street in the wake of break-ins to local cars. The camera's owner gave the footage to Haley and her family. "It was heart-wrenching. I felt helpless," says Diane. "I was thinking, 'Oh, my God!' And then, watching Clover, I was in awe. I was astounded by what she did."

Diane showed the video to a friend, who suggested they share it with a local television station. They did. And to their surprise—and somewhat disconcertingly—major media outlets and social media all over Canada and the US picked the story up. "All of a sudden we were being bombarded by phone calls and emails and these interviews," Diane says. It was an awful lot for a family that was trying to sort out a complicated medical situation, and especially for Haley. "I was overwhelmed. We were all overwhelmed," she says.

Haley had never had a seizure before that day in March, but since then she has had several. At first doctors were somewhat mystified as to the cause; they put her through myriad tests to ascertain what was going on in her brain. When the seizures began happening closer together, Haley was fast-tracked to see a neurologist. While she was in the doctor's office, Haley had another seizure, allowing the medical team to better assess what was going on and treat her with medication that is keeping her stable for the moment.

Diane still marvels at how Clover reacted to Haley collapsing. The dog was only two years old, and although she had been with the family since she was a puppy, it's a running joke in the family that she was in no way a well-trained animal. "There are no fancy tricks for Clover. She's a companion dog for our home and that's it. We tried puppy school—she got a participation award." Diane laughs.

Clover was a rescue puppy they found through an ad on Kijiji, and they were astounded when, out of the more than four hundred people who viewed the post, they were the family chosen to receive the pup. Diane compares her to a big, goofy polar bear and says they changed her name from Kiki to Clover because they had been so lucky to get her. She is a big dog, with a large, flat head, triangular ears that lie flat, dark eyes and a black nose, and when she stands on her hind feet she is almost as tall as Haley.

It may be that Clover instinctively knew to protect Haley, since the Maremma is renowned for being independent, intelligent, loyal and fiercely protective. The breed goes all the way back to the Romans, who raised these dogs to protect their livestock from predators. That being said, it's still a mystery how Clover had the instinctive wherewithal to stand in front of an oncoming vehicle until it stopped.

Diane thinks there is another possible explanation. "This dog is so loved, and she knows it," Diane says. "I really think, because of the love we've given Clover, she reciprocated. She truly did. She returned that gesture, like you would for a family member." Diane is deeply grateful for how fortunate they were that she came into their family, and smiles when she says, "She's our four-leaf clover—the dog has lived up to her name. Truly."

Tank

Taming Tics

When a sturdy, handsome service dog called Tank sidled up to Hailey and put his head in her lap, she had no idea how profoundly the American Red Labrador was about to transform her life.

Before she was partnered with Tank, Hailey was beset by dozens of tics a day—vocal and motor eruptions that she couldn't control. Her tics were so intense they caused her to have seizures, sometimes five or six times a day. It was as if her body would go into lockdown as it became overloaded by the frenetic energy. Hailey was becoming debilitated by spasms that were increasingly putting her, and those around her, at risk. Amazingly, since she and Tank have been together, Hailey hasn't had a single seizure.

Hailey was fourteen years old when she began to tic. She started to involuntarily tilt her head toward her shoulder. It was a subtle movement, but it happened repeatedly. Hailey's neurologist sent her to an involuntary movement clinic where doctors could see that Hailey was showing signs of Tourette Syndrome. When she was fifteen going on sixteen, the first tic morphed into more tics, and she started bobbing and shaking her head and making vocal clicks and whistles. For two years the tics were tolerable, but in 2020, when she was eighteen, they began to gallop out of control. Hailey's mother, Mindy, remembers it vividly. "All of a sudden, her Tourette's just blew up," she says, "and within a week they exploded, and she couldn't take care of herself."

The new tics were so rapid-fire that there were days when it was almost impossible for Hailey to even get food into her mouth. Her mother would cut up her meal and Hailey would wait for a pause between twitches and jerks to pop in a mouthful. "It makes it hard to feed yourself, especially when you're trying to hold something on a spoon and you throw it across the room, or when you're trying to hold a fork and you're stabbing a glass plate repeatedly," Hailey says. The kitchen became a particularly hazardous place. She couldn't be safely near any crockery or glasses, and the family replaced all their tableware with plastic. Despite their precautions, they narrowly averted disaster one day when a sharp knife was inadvertently left on the table. During a tic, Hailey slammed her hand down on the knife and brought it up over her head. Fortunately her mom, Mindy, managed to wrestle it out of her hand before she could inadvertently stab herself or anyone else. "You can't let her near a pot of water when her tics are bad because she has one tic, a dip tic, and if she sees a hot pot of water, she automatically wants to stick her hand in," Mindy says. "That was a very big one for us because obviously we didn't want her getting burned, so being around the stove was an absolute no."

The motor tics presented one problem, but the vocal tics were confounding in another way. In addition to clicking, whistling and sniffling, Hailey began to launch into sequences of nonsense. "I was saying things like, 'Wow, Gromit, you're a snail. You're bald,' or once I said to my dad, 'You're an ugly snail and ugly snails can't drive'—random things that just would never have come out of my mouth." She could also erupt in uncontrollable laughter, and Mindy describes how upsetting it was to witness. "Quite honestly, it was almost like she was possessed. She would have conversations with herself, and it would seem like she was having a fight between herself and her body." Hailey's illness hit a tipping point, going from barely manageable to highly problematic, and in exasperation Mindy sent a video of the onset of one such barrage to her daughter's neurologist saying, "A week ago, I had a functioning child, and this week I have a child who can't do anything." Thinking back on it, she says, "When the tics got super out of control the way they did, I'll be honest, I had a hard time dealing with it. I didn't know much about Tourette's—I knew what I'd seen on TV—and so it scared me. I was like, 'What's her life going to look like? How do we stop this from happening?'"

Hailey was diagnosed with an extreme case of Tourette Syndrome, a neurodevelopmental motor disorder whose causes aren't fully understood and for which there is no cure. Fatigue, stress and anxiety, as well as noises and visual stimuli, contribute to causing tics that, in Hailey's case, can lead to seizures. Tourette Syndrome is known to cause strangely inappropriate and sometimes dangerous behaviours.

"As it got worse, it was a lot more painful. I started punching walls. I would kick things," Hailey remembers. Her spasms were completely unpredictable and would also include paroxysms of biting, which Hailey might not sense quickly enough as she headed straight for a person's arm or shoulder. At times she has even bitten Mindy on the back. "I've had teeth prints from where she's bitten me," Mindy says. "It's the same thing if she hits you. She'll be sitting there and one second everything's fine, and then she just goes, bam! And she hits you," Mindy says. "It's absolutely the last thing she wants to do because she is a big germaphobe and the idea of biting somebody is absolutely disgusting to her. She's gone and washed her mouth out afterwards because it grosses her out. She won't even share a drink, let alone want to bite you," Mindy says. "She's the gentlest child. She wouldn't hurt fly." Hailey is uncomfortably aware of the impact of her behaviour and would apologize profusely after each onslaught, while her family reassured her it wasn't her fault.

One particularly hair-raising episode took place in the car one day. Mindy picked Hailey up after a tough day at high school, and her tics were out of control. "Sometimes her vocals go along with her motions, so she was saying, 'Lock, unlock, lock, unlock,'" Mindy says. "She was pushing a bunch of buttons, and she was hitting my lock on my door, and all of a sudden she grabbed the door handle." Hailey's tics were so severe that Mindy had to pull over and put her into the back seat with the kiddie locks turned on to keep her from causing an accident or opening a door and falling out of the car.

In 2020, Hailey was working as a counsellor at the summer camp she'd been going to since she was a child. One day her tics became so ferocious that she had her first seizure, and the camp rushed her to hospital. Mindy recalls the nightmare of getting that call from the camp. "I was forty-five minutes away, driving to the hospital, not knowing what I was going to see when I got there, how she was going to be. I cried all the way there," she remembers. But she also smiles when she remembers how Hailey greeted her upon her arrival. "I got into the room, and she looked at me and she said, 'You look worse than I do!' and she started laughing. I was like, 'You're a little smartass!'"

Despite the trauma of repeated seizures, Hailey wanted to go right back to the camp. "I just pushed through it, and I did it because I was happy to be there instead of at home being sad and mopey," she says. However, Hailey began having so many seizures it eventually became too much for the camp staff to handle, and they sent her home to look for a way to make her situation more manageable.

In a stroke of luck, Hailey discovered that noise-cancelling headphones helped stave off tics, and she wore them all day long, everywhere she went, which allowed her to return to camp. The headphones were effective but they had their drawbacks. "They were black and plastic on the outside, and they got so hot they smelled like burning plastic." Despite Hailey getting some relief with the headphones, that summer exacted a stiff emotional price, so much so that Mindy gets teary remembering it. "That was by far the worst time ever," she said.

That fall, Hailey headed off to university. She had been accepted into a demanding music program. Her instrument is the trumpet, which she had taken up when she was ten. Ironically, while audio stimuli could bring on Hailey's tics, the concentration required for her to play music suppressed them. School was demanding, and given her health concerns, the pressure was huge. She was putting in long hours and staying late on campus. The noise-cancelling headphones that had been such a godsend were becoming a liability. "So here we are with an eighteen-year-old daughter who's going to university, walking through a parking lot at nighttime, or between buildings, and she cannot hear her surroundings because she has on noise-cancelling headphones," Mindy says. "And if she does have a seizure, she's by herself. So that alone had me horrified."

Mindy is a problem solver and she began looking for a safer alternative. Hailey had noticed that when her tics were really pronounced, one way to calm them was to put the family dog, a Toy Poodle named Bubbles, onto her lap. "She would hop up on me and she would lick my hands. That's what got my mom thinking maybe a dog would help," she says. They conferred with Hailey's neurologist, who thought it was a great idea and offered to write them a doctor's note to facilitate getting a service dog in Ontario. But finding a dog trained to handle Hailey's needs was not easy. At one point Mindy thought she'd found the perfect solution, but the kennel claiming to prepare tailor-made dogs for people like Hailey turned out to be a disreputable outfit. "We were kind of crushed, because nowhere trains dogs for Tourette's," Hailey says.

And then Mindy found George Leonard, the founder and master trainer of service dogs at MSAR. He had never trained a dog for a person with Hailey's specific needs, but after several meetings by phone and Zoom with Mindy and Hailey, he agreed to put his mind to getting one ready for her.

They got down to the dollars and cents. "He gave us a ballpark figure of what the dog was going to cost, and I had to sit down because my heart almost stopped," Mindy says. Her family did not have the $33,000 it costs to acquire a dog that has had the highly specialized training necessary to be ready to go to work, so she launched an all-out campaign, from GoFundMe to a polar bear dip to raffle tickets. "I was just trying to think of absolutely everything that I could possibly do to raise the money," says Mindy, "because I didn't want to beg."

They made their goal in short order, and Mindy and Hailey headed off to Winnipeg to meet George. He had selected three possible dogs for her—a Chocolate Lab, a Labradoodle, and Tank, an American Red Lab. Tank was just shy of a year old when she met him. It was love at first sight. "Within twenty minutes of our first meeting, I had to go to the van to grab my medication out of my backpack, and he followed me along the deck and hopped up so he could watch me get my backpack. I walked back up the deck and he followed me again. He really chose me," Hailey says. "Within two days of being there he was sleeping in my bed with me. He doesn't let me go anywhere without him."

As a breed, the American Red is very calm, docile and tremendously loyal. Tank weighs in at about sixty pounds and he's a reddish blond colour, with a soft brown nose and amber eyes. He's what is known as an "anchor dog" because when he's working, he's very focused on Hailey. He leans in on her, as if to convey that he's always there and ready to support her. He walks and sits very close to her leg. She says, "He'll put his foot on my shoe just to let me know that he is there." From the get-go there was some kind of magic happening between them. Hailey's tics calmed down almost immediately, and this continued for the entire time she was with Tank at George's compound. Hailey was able to take off her headphones, keeping them around her neck but not over her ears.

This was half the battle; the other half was training. Both Tank and Hailey had to learn how to become partners. Hailey had to be taught how to train Tank to alert her to tics, which she did by teaching him that if he came to her when she made sounds imitating the noises she makes when she tics, he would get a high-value treat like a piece of chicken. Eventually it became second nature to Tank, who learned how to divert her attention to him when he sensed the onset of a tic. When Hailey focuses closely on Tank, the stimuli that cause the tic recede into the background and she becomes calm. Tank got progressively more skilled at alerting Hailey. "He would nudge me," she says. "Originally, he was very gentle. Now he is at the point where if I don't notice that he's been nudging me, or I ignore him for some reason, or he's in another room, he'll run over and jump up and push on me to make me focus on him."

Distraction and deep pressure therapy were a winning combination for Hailey. At times, Tank has to insist that Hailey listen to him, and when she does, she sits down and he lies across her, doing deep pressure therapy, which regulates her neurological system. "He distracts her so that she's not going into full-blown tics," Mindy says. "If she starts hitting something he'll come and nudge under her hand, so she pats him instead of hitting something. When she first starts to tic, if it's just mild tics, he pokes her with his nose. It's like, 'Hey, I'm here. Pet me.' If he feels that she's not listening, he'll jump at her and make sure his presence is known. Sometimes he will just hop up on her lap and lie across her." Given how petite Hailey is, and Tank's size, it's a tribute to his gentleness that these manoeuvres work.

Mindy says they don't really know exactly how having a dog works to reduce the number of tics and seizures Hailey has. "Originally, it was based on the sounds. But as they have been together, Tank has picked up on a tic before she tics. I think that's because their bond is really strong. I've never seen a person and a dog who are so in tune. It amazes me."

One big test came early on during the training. Hailey and Tank were to go into a big box store, which would have been unbearable if she had gone in alone. Such a busy, noisy place would have caused her tics to come on like a hailstorm. The lights, multitudinous sounds and temperature changes are so triggering that she would almost certainly have had a massive seizure. But on this first visit with Tank, Hailey was able to make her way through the store without panicking. She took Tank up and down the aisles, training him as they went, and she did so without losing her composure. "I was standing back watching them, and I literally had tears rolling down my face. I couldn't believe it," Mindy says, her voice catching. "Every time I tell the story, it makes me emotional, because it was the greatest moment of my life seeing this change in her."

Hailey and Tank are now inseparable. She takes him to school with her, where he attends class and has even lain beside her feet during stage performances. "I can actually go to school and learn and enjoy what I'm doing. This past year, I played in the Western Symphonic Band, and he was there for all of it. I was really, really impressed with how quickly he adapted and accepted that this was his life, because not every dog is capable or fit to be in that environment. Tank is a perfect match for a musician, especially one who plays a loud instrument like the trumpet. He'd have his ear defenders on"—noise-cancelling earphones specifically designed for dogs—"and he would just sleep through all of it," Hailey says. At times he gets annoyed by having the earphones on his head, and he knocks them off and goes back to sleep, even when the orchestra has been playing music that caused the floor to vibrate. "He's an amazing guy," she says.

Hailey has myriad other health issues. At times her heart rate spikes precipitously, which can cause her to faint. "I had one instance that was due to my blood pressure. Prior to this, Tank was very docile, very calm with his alerts, but for this he flipped out and he was like, 'You need to sit down!' He was pushing on me. He was whining. I did not feel good, I thought I was going to pass out, I was very pale. I sat down on my couch, and he went over to my mom, grabbed her sleeve, pulled her to me and made her put her hand on my knee." It was as if he was telling her she wasn't allowed to leave, Hailey says. "When the chemistry in your body changes there are different smells, which is how they pick up these things. He has picked them up naturally for me." Hailey is still going through a number of tests to see what is causing her heart rate to be so labile, and although Tank is not trained for it, he has the innate ability that medical alert dogs have to sense the onset of a medical emergency. "I've noticed he picks up her heart rate," Mindy says. "One day she was standing doing dishes and Tank alerted her. She looked at her watch and her heart rate was up to 140 [60 to 100 is normal]. Sometimes he'll let her know right beforehand, and all of a sudden, she'll start feeling dizzy and she knows she has to sit down because if not, she'll pass out." Tank is so in tune with Hailey that he senses when she's having other problems. She's been having issues with swelling in her legs, and he has intuited that applying pressure by lying across them is helpful. "It's almost like he knows her so well that he's picking up on things on his own now," Mindy says.

Hailey is very practical about how she is coping with a mountain of complicated stuff that most young people don't have to manage. "I wouldn't say I'm free of Tourette's. Some days it's very, very evident, and some days it's not. I will always live with tics because Tank isn't necessarily a magic fix. But between the medication that I'm on and him, now it's more a quirk than it is a large hindrance."

Tank has brought a sense of normalcy back to Hailey's entire family and restored peace of mind to Mindy. "I laugh much more than I used to. There was a time I would go and have a shower just so I could cry because I didn't want to cry in front of Hailey," she says. "To watch her struggle so much was hard. My parents live across the street, and I would go over and sit there and cry. I had to get out of the house for a minute, I had nowhere else to go, and I didn't want to be too far away in case anything happened. Now I feel like I can breathe again. I'm not scared every time Hailey walks out the door."

When considering how her dog has affected her life, Hailey says, "I went from not being able to leave my house, not being able to be left alone, not being able to make my own food, not being able to be independent or do anything that I really wanted to do. Any passions that I had were stripped from me. I really didn't have a whole lot of hope for what my future was going to look like, having all these issues with no way to fix them. Now, I'm a very passionate I-want-to-conquer-the-world person because I have him by my side."

Eddie

Surfacing

Shelagh's voice, a ubiquitous presence on CBC Radio for so many years, comes across the airwaves sounding like there is a smile at the other end of the microphone. But sometimes her mellifluous tones and unmistakable laugh belie an underlying truth—a long, long relationship with depression. When the metaphorical "black dog" visits itself upon her, she seeks solace in the company of the real thing.

"It seems through my whole life I've been rescued, or made better, by a dog," she says.

Long before depression infiltrated her world, Shelagh faced another health crisis. When she was a child, she came down with scarlet fever. She was only ten years old and had no idea how very serious it was—until her father, leaving Ottawa on a business trip, made her a surprising promise. "I knew I was sick because my father said to me as he was leaving, 'What can I bring you? I'll bring you anything,' and I said, 'I want a dog. I really, really, really want a dog.' I didn't think he would come home with a dog, but he did." Shelagh had read *The Incredible Journey* and was yearning for one of the book's canine characters, a Retriever named Luath. Now, miraculously, she had Honey, a Golden Retriever. Honey became a devoted companion who never left Shelagh's bedside. "She was always beside me, rammed up right against me . . . and I got better. She was absolutely the dog of my dreams."

Honey was a handful, and she was not with Shelagh's family for long. She was a big dog, too big for the kids to take out on their own, and she needed more walking than Shelagh's parents could keep up with. Eventually they decided to surrender Honey to another family. Shelagh was heartbroken, and she vowed that, someday, she would own another dog.

When she was in her twenties, under the Christmas tree she found a special delivery package from her boyfriend. Wriggling inside of tissue wrapping paper she found George, a Schnauzer puppy she describes as a "discount dog," complete with a rib that stuck out. It was the beginning of her Schnauzer period. She would become the owner of many more: Gracie, Strauss, Poppy, and eventually Sam, all little castoffs that came to her because they were unwanted.

Shelagh was headed for some tough times; for years she rode a roller coaster of mental health ups and downs. As a young woman, she was repeatedly misdiagnosed, one doctor dismissing her symptoms as PMS and putting her on hormones that just messed with her system even more. In 2003, when she was forty-seven, she crashed in a complete breakdown and had to take a six-month leave from her very public job as a national radio host. From the outside it looked as though Shelagh had it all . . . but on the inside she was floundering. She hid it well.

Even her own mother, with whom she had a very complicated relationship, upon learning that she suffered from depression, was mystified, citing Shelagh's wonderful upbringing and her big job and big life. But as Shelagh observes, "depression is an equal opportunity thief."

That depression lasted for months. She had fallen hard. "I couldn't talk. I lay on my bed all day long, just staring up at the ceiling." The irony that she, a radio host, lost her voice certainly did not go unnoticed. "I could make noise. I could squawk a little," she says with a wry laugh, "but it was very raspy, and I just couldn't bring it back. That added more to the overall feeling of depression, because I thought, 'Maybe it's never coming back and it's kind of all I've got.'"

During this time, Strauss and Poppy the Schnauzers were her closest company, her safeguards. "I had days where I was just lying on the floor of the bathroom. And if that happened, the dogs were there," she says, remembering that Strauss and Poppy never strayed from her side, no matter where she was. "These two dogs were like sentries. There was one on my left side, one on my right side. I knew they were there; I couldn't say anything to them, but I could pat them, and they never left my side except to go out for walks and to get their food."

As a public figure, Shelagh's working life was all about being scrutinized and living up to expectations. At the time, she was hosting a morning radio show that had some serious growing pains, and she was feeling the weight of it all. But Poppy and Strauss provided Shelagh with their undemanding presence and unconditional love, and she felt a profound relief in the simplicity of her dogs' devotion. "There isn't that weight of expectation except, 'When are we going for a walk?' or 'When's dinner?' It's so simple," she says.

Shelagh began taking the dogs out for walks in her west end Toronto neighbourhood. "I was being pulled along, because my dogs were never dogs that heeled"—she smiles—"by these two Schnauzers and feeling they wouldn't let me fall." At some primal level, the dogs worked a magic that was as helpful as any other kind of therapy, and gradually Shelagh began to rally. "The fact that dogs need to be walked means you have to be in motion and being in motion helps so much," she says, adding, "I remember winter kind of slipping away and feeling maybe I could do this. I could get out and put one foot in front of another."

Fast-forward to another period in Shelagh's life, when she had moved to British Columbia and was doing a show there. Two months after the death of her Schnauzer Sam, she and her husband Charlie found themselves at the Nanaimo SPCA looking for a new pooch. There they found a tiny puppy called Eddie, a bristly brown terrier mutt that had come into the shelter bruised, swollen and abandoned. From the minute she set eyes on him, Shelagh vowed he would never again have another bad day. And, she says, he hasn't.

Shelagh tells a poignant story about how Eddie helped her to help some shell-shocked students. In the fall of 2019, she was chancellor at the University of Victoria when there was a tragic bus accident. Two students died and seventeen were injured when the bus they were travelling on during a university field trip rolled down an embankment in a rainstorm. A few days after the accident, a commemorative gathering was held on campus and two therapy dogs were in attendance. Shelagh brought Eddie too. "He's not a therapy dog, but I was chancellor at the time, so I used my chancellor privilege," she remembers. "One of the students was back at the back of the room just staring out into space and that's who Eddie went to—the person whose need might have been impossible to express, you know? Eddie does this thing where he really whams up against you and just doesn't leave, and I was so proud of him that day. Everybody loved him and he made people a bit happier that day, under the circumstances."

Thinking about her dogs and their unwavering service in her times of need, Shelagh says, "Every dog I've had except for George has been a rescue. But we're the ones that need the rescuing, you know?" And she observes that, with all of her dogs, "it was like they had a job to do. And I think dogs like to have a job, whether it's guarding against the ferocious postal worker or cats." And she laughs—that Shelagh laugh.

Oakee

Balancing Act

Khiem learned early that the world was a hostile place for a little boy like himself. When he was eleven years old, his family emigrated to Canada from South Vietnam and moved into a primarily white suburban neighbourhood in Scarborough. Khiem spoke no English and was one of a handful of South Asian kids in his school. He was pushed around by kids who saw him as different; he remembers the bullying being especially difficult in grades 7, 8 and 9.

At home, his family was riddled with tension. Khiem remembers feeling that his mother's mental health made her difficult to be around and that his father could be a capricious man. Khiem would wake each morning wondering if he might be caned by his father.

Dogs had been an integral part of Khiem's young life. In Vietnam, his grandfather kept six or seven German Shepherds as protection and as much-loved family pets. Khiem remembers proudly rescuing a litter of street dog puppies from some bushes near his home and keeping two as his very own. When he had to leave to come to Canada, his family's circumstances meant having a dog wasn't possible, but still, he longed for one. When he was in grade 13 and he heard of a family selling puppies from their backyard, he couldn't resist. He scrounged up forty dollars and bought one, a beautiful Siberian Husky. Khiem named him Blue because of the colour of his eyes.

Heartbreakingly, Blue came to a tragic end. Neighbourhood kids threw some poisoned meat into Khiem's backyard as a prank, and when the dog suffered brain seizures, Khiem had to make the decision to have him put down. The dog was only six years old, and it was crushingly painful. Khiem was never able to puzzle out exactly which kid had thrown the meat, but he remembers vividly the "horrible anger" he felt about the cruelty of it. In the wake of Blue's death, Khiem recalls shutting down, becoming isolated in his pain. "I was grieving so I said, 'No, I'm not ready to have another pet in my life when I know I can't take care of my own self right now. I'm not balanced enough, stable enough. Why should I bring the next pet into my life?' It took years for me to figure myself out before I committed and got myself another dog."

While he was figuring himself out, Khiem, who is a serious outdoors person, embraced an itinerant lifestyle, seeking adventure in places other than his home turf. He would get in his car and take off, always wishing he had a dog along for the ride.

When he was just shy of his thirtieth birthday, Khiem felt he was ready to become a dog owner again, and he began looking for the right canine companion. He needed a dog that could match his own boundless energy and could handle his solo trips into the back country, canoeing, hiking, biking and camping.

He loved Australian Shepherds, cattle dogs that are high maintenance and hugely energetic, but he also wanted a dog with a little more gravitas, one that wouldn't be overwhelmed by the challenges, and even dangers, they might encounter. When Khiem heard that Aussie Shepherd/Black Lab puppies were being given away at a farm an hour and a half away, he jumped in his car on Christmas Eve and made a beeline straight there. He sat among the puppies and watched how they related to him. Some clustered around him, but one diffident little fellow was quite happy to go his own way, and that's the one Khiem chose. He called him Oakee—which he made up by contracting the names of two things special to him, his Oakley sunglasses and his Jeep Cherokee.

Oakee had a black and white coat with floppy ears, and the white markings above his eyes gave him the appearance of having eyebrows, adding personality to his happy face. Australian Shepherds, bred to be herding dogs, are high energy, which made him an excellent match for Khiem; both thrived on being active and in the outdoors. And there was more to it than that. Oakee "got" what was going on when Khiem became a bit off-balance.

Khiem says this was the dog that saved his life, and Khiem's partner Mel says she thinks that without Oakee, Khiem would have been headed down a bad path. The corrosive impact of childhood trauma and years of bullying by his peers was something Khiem carried quietly. As a teenager he felt it was better for him to exit his emotionally volatile household than to stay, but hanging out in the street presented opportunities for getting in trouble. He did have one outlet, though. Sports, especially soccer, helped divert him away from what he describes as inner rage. Still, when provoked one time too many, he would move into a "red zone" of fury when things didn't go his way, or outright road rage when he was in the car.

Oakee somehow intuitively understood how to help manage these times. When they were in the car, Oakee would sense when Khiem's stress levels were on the upswing. He would leave his usual perch in the back of the SUV, get up behind Khiem, lean in close to him, and put his paw on his shoulder. If that didn't help, he would lick the side of his head. That was usually enough, but when it wasn't, he would nip, and if that didn't work, he'd nip hard.

When Khiem became agitated in other situations, Oakee's ability to read his body language was so acute it was as if he could feel Khiem's racing heartbeat. He would run circles around him as Aussies do when they are herding cattle, trying to drive him away from his anger. If that didn't work, Oakee would insert himself between Khiem and the person with whom he was having an issue. Or he'd interject by barking and pawing at Khiem, and depending on the intensity of the situation, the pawing would escalate from a light tap to one strong enough to break Khiem's skin. No matter what, Oakee was determined to keep his human out of trouble, and it worked.

Khiem had dreamed of taking Oakee to the west coast where they could hike and spend time outdoors, but that got put on hold when he met Mel. Khiem has Oakee to thank for filling a void in his romantic life too. Their love affair bloomed when they met while walking their dogs. Eventually, Khiem and Mel decided they should pursue his dream together. They packed the dogs into the car and resettled on the Sunshine Coast in British Columbia. In their first year on the coast, they explored fifty-two different hikes with the dogs. Oakee's need for lots of strenuous exercise dovetailed perfectly with Khiem's need to be active to maintain his own equilibrium.

When Khiem began a new job working with people with brain injuries, he discovered another of Oakee's inborn abilities. One of Khiem's clients was a young man who had suffered a drug-related stroke and, as a result, was having a significant number of seizures. Khiem knew the client loved dogs, so he introduced him to Oakee and they began going on walks. The client's seizures ranged from light to massive, and sometimes landed him in hospital for days. Without any training, Oakee began to anticipate when a seizure was about to come on, and by licking the young man's hand he could help bring him out of one. For the three or four years Khiem worked with this client, he brought Oakee along to their meetings. When Oakee was with them, the client's seizure activity dropped to almost zero. It was another gift from Oakee, making Khiem's professional life even more gratifying.

Oakee died in 2020 after a full and happy life. Khiem and Mel still live on the west coast, and Khiem is out on the trails pretty well every day with his dog Kai, a massive white Dogo Argentino. Of all the places Oakee hiked with Khiem and Mel, they think his favourite was a provincial park overlooking the Georgia Strait. Every time they made their way through the park, Oakee would linger on one particular ridge, looking out on the world as if he had discovered its secret. This is where they scattered his ashes into the wind.

Zeus

Two Close Calls

Alex is a petite blonde whose pixieish mien belies her age. She is fifty-seven, and an intrepid and gifted actor, writer and playwright. Her work in theatre has taken her around the world—which is impressive in and of itself, but is also remarkable because Alex is completely blind.

Remarkable, too, is her first story of how her dog saved her life—long before she began losing her sight.

Alex was three years old when her family moved to a small farm, thirty-two acres of bucolic countryside. They lived in a big white house at the end of a long lane, and even though Alex and her older brother Matt were small children, they were given free rein to roam the property. It was 1969, and in the country, it was not uncommon for children to go outside with little supervision and few limits to where they could play. Alex remembers that her folks were especially relaxed about this, the polar opposite of helicopter parents. She jokes, "My parents sold the helicopter and fired the pilot." Alex was a mischievous kid, too young to have developed a sense of danger, yet there was danger everywhere on a rural property and she was often getting into some misadventure.

Behind the house was a big old barn, a dark and exciting place to explore, where the kids loved to play. One morning Alex and Matt were riding their tricycles inside the barn and their dog Dandy, a German Shepherd/hound mix, was with them. As Alex's trike rolled over a section of the barn floor, the old floorboards gave way beneath her and her trike fell through, front wheel first. Only the tricycle's wider back wheels prevented her from falling right through onto the lower level of the barn. She remembers dangling from the front wheel while her brother went into the house to find their mother. Matt, who was two years older than Alex, was only five years old and was far too young to understand the import of what had just happened. Neither child recognized the peril of Alex's situation. "That's the beauty of being a child," she says. "You don't realize what's wrong until you've had something bad happen, and at that moment, all I was doing was hanging on to a wheel."

While Alex doesn't recall feeling frightened, she does remember her arm getting very tired and wondering what would happen if she let go. Then she remembers deciding to let go, landing painfully on top of a wall, possibly a cement stall divider, and it hurt. "Then I toppled over. I could hear my dog barking in the distance, and I could hear this big engine. I didn't really know what was going on. I had fallen into a pile of corn, which felt kind of nice." Alex had landed in a piece of farm machinery that pulverized corn with a high-speed rotating blade and hammers, and as she remembers it, "The machine was grinding the corn up, basically making niblets. I was about to become a niblet." She laughs.

A local farmer was working at the very machine Alex had fallen into. It was loud, and he didn't hear or see Alex coming through the floor above. Dandy had witnessed the fall through the barn floor and ran outside the barn, down to the lower level where the farmer was mulching with the machine. She barked at him so insistently that he was alarmed and turned off the machine.

The rest is a blur for Alex, although she does have scattershot memories. "I remember being pulled out. And I remember my mother showing up. And the next thing I remember is being in the back of a car, while the two of them, the farmer and my mother, were in the front seat talking as they drove me to the hospital because I had hurt myself by falling on that wall the way I did. They were concerned that I had a spinal injury or something, because I couldn't walk."

It turned out that Alex was fine. No spinal injury, no head injury. And she had Dandy to thank for not being macerated by the corn grinder.

"I don't know how my dog had the intelligence or instinct to go down to the basement of the barn and bark at the farmer. Dogs are amazing that way—they smell danger. I've had guide dogs and I know how sensitive they are to how I am feeling, because it has affected how they guide me. If I'm upset about something, they get nervous, they don't walk confidently, they don't guide well." Alex believes that dogs are alert to instances when people are at sixes and sevens, or when they are in danger, and she thinks this may have been what caused Dandy to run to find a human who could do something to help. And when Alex thinks about Dandy's persistent barking and the sound of the big engine stopping, she has absolute clarity about this: "My dog *actually* saved my life, not metaphorically or spiritually, but truly!"

Many decades down the road, when Alex was in theatre school, her vision began to deteriorate. She was diagnosed with retinitis pigmentosa, a rare genetic eye disease, and began to lose her peripheral vision. Incrementally she lost more and more of her sight, and by the time she was thirty, she'd lost enough of her sight to need a service dog. In 1997 she got Gyra, a petite, ginger-coloured Golden Retriever from a dog-training school in California. It changed her life for the better.

Navigating the world while blind is challenging and, at times, downright hazardous. The simplest tasks, like going to work or the doctor, using public transit or going for a walk, can be daunting. Alex's peripatetic lifestyle intensified her need for assistance, and while there was never any doubt that she would find ways to pursue her interests, things became markedly more manageable when she and Gyra began to go through daily life together.

One day when she and Gyra were out and about, Alex had an epiphany about the psychosocial importance of her relationship with her dog, and why it was having such a profound impact on her well-being. On this day, she and Gyra simply made a stop at the grocery store. Gyra had guided Alex from home to the shop, and they made their way through the store together as Alex picked up the things they each needed for dinner that night. Gyra brought Alex home safely. Alex prepared dinner and made sure they both got fed.

Before Alex had Gyra, she had relied on people to take her to the store, help her shop, walk her home, unload and put things away. They would then leave, and Alex was on her own. Because her human helpers didn't rely on Alex for help, it was a one-way dependency, which often left her feeling somewhat less than equal with her friends, despite how well meaning they were. When Alex relied on her dog, it was two-way. Each relied on the other for the simplest but most necessary things. As she says, "Basically, she kept me alive and I kept her alive." This deceptively simple example reveals a partnership that she otherwise hadn't had as a blind person. "Becoming blind was a hard thing in terms of relationships. I thought everyone else was of more value to me than I was to them because everyone else was taking care of me," Alex says. "It was a beautiful moment for me."

There have been two important service dogs in Alex's life—Gyra and Zeus. Zeus was a sturdy Black Lab she got from a dog school when she lived in the United Kingdom some years later. He was Alex's closest companion for eight and a half years. Zeus was a saint of an animal and was adept at dealing with the complex needs of an internationally active actor and producer who was in and out of so many different environments.

But it was after a domestic accident that Zeus really shone as Alex's protector. Alex was alone in her home in London, and she heard Zeus barking to come in from the backyard. Alex went to let him in, tripped and pitched headlong down the stairs, cracking her head on the front door and knocking herself out. From where he was in the backyard, Zeus was able to see through sliding glass doors to Alex's crumpled body where it lay at the bottom of the stairs beside the front door. As Alex says, he "went ballistic." His barking alarmed a neighbour, who called the police. When the police arrived, they banged on the front door, but hearing the very agitated Zeus, they went into the neighbour's backyard and then jumped the fence to Alex's yard. From there, they were able see into the house where Alex was lying in a heap on the floor, and they came in through the back door.

Alex had a concussion and was taken to hospital, where she recovered. She learned later that, if not for Zeus's barking, the police would have kicked in the front door where Alex was lying, which would have brought the door down hard on top of her, quite possibly causing more extensive injuries.

Zeus protected Alex's physical safety every day. He kept her from falling into holes or walking into poles. But as importantly, he was a safeguard to her overall well-being. "The way people related to me when I had a dog was better," she explains. "I felt that people saw me as a more glued together human being, less vulnerable, less needy. I think also there was a kind of positivity that a dog carried into a room with me."

Alex describes at times feeling pitied or patronized and says a dog can bridge the gap between her and a sighted person. She describes dogs as connectors and mitigators of isolation. "I mean, people go into a park, and everybody knows the dog's name. They create community." She laughs as she adds, "And my white cane unfortunately does not create community. It does the opposite."

As an actor, Alex thinks in terms of story. When she's onstage she has some measure of control over how people see her, because she becomes the part she is playing. When she compares that to life offstage, she says, "If you're blind and entering a space, you sit down and people are looking at you and thinking, 'Oh, she's blind.' That's it, you're blind and that's your story. When you're in a play, you're part of a bigger story." Alex has learned that having a dog with her when she's offstage means that she can feel part of a bigger, better story. For her, that is life-saving.

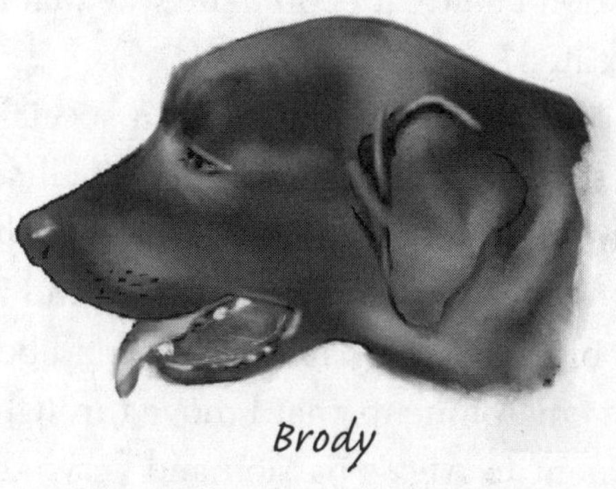

Brody

Freedom Found

A year before Alex had to retire her beloved Zeus, she began to apply to dog schools. She had timed his retirement for the fall of 2018, and hoped she'd have another dog a few months later. It didn't work out that way . . . instead it took five arduous years to find a new guide dog. Alex applied to many schools, all over the US and Canada, sometimes with dissatisfying outcomes. Some schools had impossibly long wait-lists. One school sent her home with a dog ill-suited to the city. And another school mixed up her personal information with another blind candidate's and gave Alex a dog that was too small for her, and she had to come home empty-handed. One dog was temperamentally a bad match and was walking Alex too close to traffic. Rather than offering support, the school pulled the dog. "The matching process between a blind person and their dog is so important. And that is one of the reasons that makes some schools really good and some schools not good at all, because they don't take enough time to properly match a person," Alex says. She adds that "they don't all treat people the way that I expect blind people to be treated."

Because of Alex's lifestyle, she needs a special kind of dog. "I travel a lot. I work in the arts. I move to all sorts of different places for work. I don't have your typical profile for a blind person needing a dog. I also live in a big city, and it takes a very particular kind of dog to work in a big city and be adaptable to all the different environments that I move through."

It is a testament to Alex's passion and verve that she maintained this lifestyle while, and after, losing her vision. And it is a testament to the dogs she has had that they have been able to adapt so seamlessly to constant change.

The years when Alex was longing for a guide dog had a significant impact on her physical and mental health. She became anxious and depressed. "I spent many of those years needing antidepressants, rightly so." She felt vulnerable and like she was shrinking. "Without a dog, I feel like I make myself as small as I possibly can because at the same time, I feel way too visible, which is why I make myself small. I walked around feeling like I'm a target. When you move through the world shuffling along, not feeling particularly safe, at a speed that is so slow it gives you the message that you're weak and you're old or you're not capable, it's a psychologically very difficult way of being."

Without a dog, Alex had to brush up on her cane skills. "Lots of people are good with their white canes, way better than I was. I got better over the five years, but because I'd had a dog for so long I was just a disaster," she says. Going out into the world on her own was never comfortable, and often stressful, leaving her feeling chronically vulnerable. "Honestly, I would come home, and I would think I needed to celebrate the fact that I'm alive.

I was amazed every time nothing bad had happened, or if something bad did happen, that I got home okay. I was always certain there was going to be a guy following me through that door, because so many guys were following me around."

In January of 2024, Alex got word that she had been accepted to The Seeing Eye dog school in Morristown, New Jersey. This time the school and Alex were very well suited. "I had heard there was one person in my circle who had gotten a dog from there, and it was a successful experience. But you never know. Honestly, it's such a roll of the dice when a blind person gets on a plane or a train or bus and goes to a training centre. You really don't know what you're getting into. I can tell you that it can be terrible, but this place was the dream."

Alex was among a coterie of twenty blind people who were there to train with a new dog. She spent the first few days getting oriented to the school protocols while the school observed her to assess which dog would best suit her needs. "You spend those first few days on pins and needles, wondering who's going to be your best friend for the rest of its life, and a big chunk of your own life." Alex gets teary as she recalls her first encounter with her new dog. "It makes me emotional talking about it," she says. "When your dog comes through that door and runs over and licks your face and does little circles in front of you, it is like the whole world has just opened up, because they change your life. They really do."

Alex had been matched with a remarkable dog named Brody, an unusually gentle dog—one-quarter Golden Retriever and three-quarters Black Lab, with a gleaming jet-black coat and ebony almond-shaped eyes. "Everybody says he's really, really handsome, which I know he is," Alex says, and adds what she sees in her mind's eye. "He has a big head. That's the thing

I noticed most. It's like it's fallen off a bear onto a dog's body. He's got kind of funny proportions, which I love. He's got character. He's got big paws and his little nose is still very much like a puppy nose. It's very soft and it's very wet. And he doesn't like it when I play with it," she says, laughing.

Bringing a guide dog home presents its own kind of challenges. A good six months are needed to cement the training and ensure the human-canine bond is solid and reliable. Alex was relatively new to her neighbourhood, and it was her job to introduce Brody to an area chockablock with high-rise towers that are home to dozens of dogs. Brody and Alex were teaching each other—Brody to understand Alex's commands, and Alex to figure out how to stickhandle their relationship to the outside world. "The blind person remains the captain of the team. The dog doesn't decide when to cross the road. They don't decide when the light is green. They don't decide that we're going out the door and turn left and right to get to the grocery store. They listen to the blind person. The blind person gives them all their instructions. It's a lot of work, but it is the best relationship! So interdependent. So powerful."

While it was instant love when Alex and Brody met at the school, their arrival in Toronto almost derailed their working relationship. Day one was traumatic. In the early evening, Alex took Brody out to do his business on the lawn beside the apartment building where they live, and Brody was attacked by another dog. That dog's owner—inattentive, distracted or indifferent—did nothing despite Alex's call for help. Once she let out a roar, the owner pulled the dog off Brody and peeled off, leaving Alex to deal with the fallout. The memory still unsettles her. "The worst thing that could happen is for a guide dog to come home and be attacked within twenty-four hours," she says, "because it immediately establishes to the dog, or could establish, that where they are isn't safe." Alex learned from the school that an attack like that could ruin a guide dog permanently, especially one that is so freshly on the job. Fortunately, Brody has recovered, but he was rattled; Alex says, "I've got to say, his guiding was not great for the first few weeks after that."

It is a tribute to Brody, and to the bond that exists between the two of them, that he has managed to settle into his responsibilities. In a densely populated city, multitudinous distractions crop up during every single walk. For example, people have yelled and cursed at them to get out of the way, which is intimidating, to say the least.

Alex lives half a block away from a massive 398-acre park in the west end of Toronto. Proximity to the green space was a big part of why she moved into the neighbourhood. Without a dog, however, the park was inaccessible to her. She describes the park as "a teasing little child" that mocked her because she couldn't go in by herself. "I was thinking about this yesterday. I came home with Brody. We'd gone into High Park for a little walk. We came back home and I thought, I moved to this High Park area and everybody was saying, 'Oh, you're going to love it. There's the park. So much fun, you go for walks, da da da . . .' Everybody talked about the park, and I just thought, I'm miserable. There's a park and I can't do anything with it, unless somebody comes over and takes me into it, which I appreciate, but it was almost worse to be near this beautiful environment that was out of my reach. Then yesterday I came home, and I thought, Oh my God, the park is mine. It's finally mine, and it's because of Brody. He's given me the park and so much more. These guide dogs make the world a place that belongs to you as well as to other people."

In the months since Alex and Brody were matched, they've met, and handled, numerous challenges, including Brody becoming gravely ill from eating something he shouldn't have. Brody has helped Alex to ride the subway again, though he's still having to learn how to board the train quickly enough that the doors don't shut on him. Before Brody, Alex had shied away from the subway after she was assaulted by an unstable woman as she came out of a station. Brody gives her a renewed sense of safety, and Alex is convinced that she would not have been attacked if she'd had her dog with her.

Overall, Alex's mood has lifted in the months she's had Brody. She laughs more readily, and she is more mobile in unexpected ways. "I walk faster with Brody than I probably would if I could see, which is hilarious. It's almost a little bit like sailing, and I love it. I get to move at a pace that really appeals to my personality, and that feels good. It feels right. I don't feel like I'm in the wrong body, which I did when I was using a cane."

Asked whether Brody has saved her life, Alex considers the question in the context of gaining a new equilibrium. "I often felt that I was just a vessel that received other people's kindness when people were helping me out. As nice as that is, you can start to feel like you have nothing to offer. I do have things to offer. In that way, I think Brody has brought balance back into my life."

Tatala

Muzzling Torment

Jerry grew up in an extremely violent household. Two things got him through his childhood . . . his much-adored grandmother, whom he called Bubbe, and a dog named Damian.

Jerry spent his young years in Bedford-Stuyvesant, a neighbourhood in Brooklyn, New York. "We were the only white family amidst Spanish and Black, and it was all low-income. It was the ghettos. I remember they were rat-infested, drug-addicted slums where every day was a challenge to survive," he says.

It was a tough world for a kid, made worse because Jerry ping-ponged from one episode of ill treatment to another. "Both of my parents are deaf, and my father was very, very, very abusive." His father would beat him with a belt, and his mother was complicit in the violence. When he was fourteen years old, he ran away from home with another kid his age. They were picked up by a beat cop late that night and brought into the precinct, where Jerry was instructed to call his family to let them know where he was. "My father walks into the police station. My father is a milkman, six foot two, a muscular, tough guy. The first thing he does when he sees me, he yells and punches me in the face, and I do a somersault to the floor. And I'll never forget one cop snickering to another cop, 'I can see why that kid left home.'" His voice still registers incredulity that a father would do such a thing to a kid and that no one stepped in to protect him.

Jerry coped with the daily violence by hurling invective at his father as soon as he turned his back, which he got away with because his father was deaf. "I grew up learning screaming was good, and I would scream at everybody. This is a serious problem I have. As soon as I would get upset with you, I'd say, 'You're such a fucking idiot,' and that doesn't work when you get older." Learning to manage his emotions is an ongoing undertaking for Jerry, and dogs have played a significant role in that process. When he was growing up, he saw what violence did to dogs. "The animals where I grew up, the dogs and the strays, were all emaciated and as soon as they saw a human being, they ran to the high hills because they knew if they got caught, they were going to be abused terribly."

As a kid, Jerry's grandmother's home became an outpost of safety. He would hide there, seeking a moratorium from the violence at home. He refers to his Bubbe's house as his "safe spot." She would shower him with love and good food, and she referred to him endearingly in Yiddish as "tatala," meaning "dear boy." Jerry also found solace in the company of Damian, a foundling mutt he cherished. "I could pet him, and, like my grandmother, he was safe. He gave me love, and he made me feel good."

Eventually Jerry cut off all ties with his parents and his siblings, and, after a trip to Toronto, made a move that would change his life even more. “I came up with a girlfriend on my first visit outside of the slums, and I just fell in love with the country. I couldn’t believe that people live this way. The streets were clean!” He made the decision to emigrate and has now lived in Canada longer than he lived in the United States.

Jerry was born in the mid-1950s. He has a head of grey hair and an impressive grey beard, and when he puts on his sunglasses, he looks as though he’s about to jump on a Harley motorcycle and take off. As a young man he was living the high life, quite literally. “I was into everything. I was living with this girl; we were swingers right before AIDS. I stopped when AIDS came.” It was the era of nightclubs and parties and lots of drugs. He was a devotee of cocaine, about which he is unapologetic, and he made lots of money doing everything from trading stocks and owning a collection agency to opening a fitness studio. “I never made more money than when I was doing coke,” he says.

In the early days of COVID, Jerry became mysteriously sick. Doctors couldn’t figure out what was going on. “I just started getting weaker and weaker and weaker and weaker and weaker.” Eventually he, the super-fit gym rat, had trouble walking. His illness seemed to be on a relentless path, and he became so physically fragile he was bedridden. He was tested for everything from leukemia to heart failure to Parkinson’s disease, but his condition remained a mystery. Jerry became so distressed and depressed he canvassed his doctor about seeking assisted suicide if things didn’t improve.

But somehow, despite thinking he might die, an idea kept running through his mind, like an earworm he couldn’t ignore.

He confided to his wife that he wanted to get a dog. "My wife said, 'You can't walk,' and I said, 'I know. I'll find a little dog—a Chihuahua that will shit in the house in kitty litter, but I need to have one.'"

Jerry and his wife, Catherine, live in a condo in the inner city where you can't just open the door and let the dog out. Catherine overcame her concerns about the possibility that she would be primarily responsible for caring for the dog, and Jerry began to apply to rescue organizations. He wrote letters and filled out forms, apprising each organization of his few conditions. "I needed a dog that didn't bark because of my neighbours; I needed a dog that needed very little walking because I couldn't walk; I didn't want a violent dog because if it was biting it would be hard for me, because I was weak." It took six months, and several disheartening rejections, before Jerry got word that one rescue organization had found just the right dog for him. According to the documentation Jerry received, she had been emancipated from an abusive soccer player in the Dominican Republic. She had also been hit by a car. "She's had a terrible life," Jerry says. "When I first got her, she was afraid of everything. I've never had a dog like that. All my dogs were tough and dominant. This was my first passive, scaredy-cat dog."

Jerry wanted to name his new-found friend after his grandmother, but because she was a religious woman, he conferred with a rabbi, who advised against naming a dog after a human being. "So I did the next best thing and named her Tatala," he says. "I'm so glad I did, because sometimes I call her that name and I think of my Bubbe, and I go, 'Bubbe, I miss you.'" His critics objected to his name choice, saying he couldn't give the dog this name because it's meant for a boy. "I said, 'My dog is gender neutral! She's okay with it and I'm okay with it,'" he says, laughing.

Tatala was a little bigger than the Chihuahua Jerry originally had in mind. She looks like a Jack Russell Terrier, with a white stripe running up her brown and black snout, and patches of black and brown in her white coat. When she arrived in Canada, she was so traumatized she cowered in her crate. It was three weeks before Jerry saw Tatala wag her tail for the first time. He still gets excited talking about it. "It was like pizza! It was like getting laid! It was like the best sex of my life. It was such a wonderfully rewarding experience!"

The rescue organization had mistakenly assumed that she would be a sedentary dog, but Jerry was seeing her transform right before his eyes. "Because she was so scared and abused, they thought that she doesn't need to run," Jerry says. "I started taking her to the park and I saw that my dog loves to run, my dog loves to play. My dog is energetic. And she made me walk. I had to keep up with her and I was improving and improving," he adds. "I was doing things I would never have done without her. I started to get better because of her; this dog made me go further."

Jerry and Tatala, two wounded warriors, began metamorphosing in tandem. "I felt very alone in my fight against everything, even though I had my wife here. Now I don't feel alone. People can say it's just a dog. It's not just a dog. It's much, much more to me. It's a relationship. She depends on me, and I depend on her, and we're a team," he says. "When you're down and out, you need things around you that make you feel needed. When a person feels needed, and not dependent on others, they wind up improving. It's just the way we are as human beings. And a dog gives it to you like nothing else," Jerry continues. "Listen,

I'm fucked up from my childhood. She's been abused for her entire childhood. It's going to take a long time, if ever, for her to be 100 percent. We're just shooting for 80 percent."

Tatala is also helping Jerry recalibrate how he responds to stress and anger. "What I do is, I begin asking her to come here and I just touch her. By doing that it enables me to calm down, get a clear perspective." The magic Tatala works with Jerry, helping him manage his emotions and behaviour, is due, in part, to the way in which contact with a dog helps him regulate his nervous system.

Jerry says it's not just the physical connection that comes from touch that is healing scars he carries from his childhood. "I look at it like she's my shrink. She helps me bring my emotions into check and my feelings into perspective. And she does that by bringing out the best in me, the way a shrink does. She permits me to use my own intelligence to come up with different answers, because she puts me in a different place emotionally. She makes me think better," he says. "I always tell people she's my rescue dog and I'm her rescue human. I mean, this is a two-way street. Rescue dog, rescue human." Jerry concludes, "Tatala means everything to me."

PJ

Housebound

For years, social anxiety loomed over Jenna, anxiety so extreme that she became its hostage. "I'm afraid of people, essentially," she says. "I always felt really, really alone, like I had no idea what was going on." When she was in her mid-twenties, she spent three years virtually housebound.

Jenna has been afflicted with a constellation of maladies for many years, but it wasn't until she was a young adult that she began to fully understand why. "I didn't get my diagnosis until I was twenty-one, but I knew something was wrong, something was different, *I* was different." Learning that she has autism spectrum disorder brought into focus why she felt so frightened and vulnerable in the outside world, and why she didn't fit in with her contemporaries. It's quite common for women to be diagnosed with autism much later than their male counterparts, but that doesn't make living with the symptoms any easier.

Jenna says she was very young when she began to experience inexplicable bullying and cruelty. "That began pretty much as soon as I started school," she explains, "and by first grade, you could start to see people were not treating me the same. The older I got, the more pronounced my issues seemed to become, or the more obvious they became. Throughout the rest of elementary school and high school and college, I was bullied."

Jenna is impressively self-possessed in her assessment of what it was like growing up as a marginalized child. She says she wasn't physically bullied, but there were plenty of verbal insults. "Sticks and stones might break my bones—but bones can heal, and they heal stronger. Words, you remember those for a really long time."

When Jenna is interacting one-on-one, or in a small group, she is direct, smart and charming. But she says she is often slightly out of sync in everyday exchanges in larger groups of people. When she interacted with groups of her peers, it was often achingly awkward. "I looked like I was a little bit crazy because I couldn't follow along with the conversation. And as smart as I know I am, in situations like that, I can't follow. Any time they're talking, they'll ask me a question and I'm five or six sentences behind everyone, so I'm like, 'Wait, wait, give me second, let me process where we are.'"

After two painful years in post-secondary programs, Jenna gave up and retreated into herself. She was living with her mother, where she felt safe, but being cooped up inside for years on end added to her isolation and depression. Even going out for a walk was complicated. Just a glance from a passerby could set off a reaction, and Jenna would become overwhelmed by negative thoughts about people she encountered on the street. "I'd be walking down the street and I would see somebody walking and they'd just sort of glance at you and then they keep walking. Most people that would be, 'Yeah, they're just having their day, whatever.' But for me, it was like they probably looked at me and thought, you know, I'm lazy, I'm probably a little bit weird. Like, all of these negatives."

Jenna has always found it easier to be around animals than people, especially dogs. "I don't feel like I have to worry about what they're thinking because dogs are very open about how they feel. They don't try and hide it."

Jenna's life took a sharp turn for the better in the spring of 2020, thanks to a canine import from Central America. One evening, she and her mother found themselves standing at the arrivals gate at Toronto International Airport shortly after midnight, waiting to collect a thirty-pound miracle who had just made a thirteen-hour flight from Costa Rica to Canada.

When PJ emerged, a ball of black and white spots and speckles, golden eyes and slightly cockeyed ears (one bent, one straight), it was love at first sight. "That was absolutely an incredible moment. I cried, because for me, when I saw her, she was so small but she was so beautiful and she was so sweet right from the beginning," Jenna says. "As soon as we picked her up at the airport, it didn't even take five minutes before I started feeling better, and within twenty-four hours we had already gone on a walk and we had snuggled."

Jenna had begun her hunt for a dog, in part, because of her relationship with her mother's dog, Teddy, with whom she had been very close. "I was closer to him than he was to me. He was Mum's, for sure, but he was a fantastic little dog," Jenna remembers. "He was rescued at the age of seven, and we had him for only three years, but he was, more or less, as perfect a dog as a dog can get without being playful, because he didn't know how to play. He was really sweet." When Teddy died, Jenna and her mother decided Jenna would benefit from having her own dog.

It was during COVID and people were scrambling for dogs. Rescue dogs were in especially high demand, so it took time. "Mum and I started looking for dogs that had certain qualities that would be good as a service dog. And we applied for a couple of dogs, and a couple of rescues, and heard nothing back from any of them." But then, through friends, they found PJ.

Serendipitously, PJ had been found running loose in the streets of San José by a veterinarian who works with a Costa Rican animal rescue organization. The vet happened to hear a commotion outside her window in the middle of the night. When she realized it was a young female dog who was in her first heat, being pursued by a group of eager male dogs, she ran out in her pyjamas, scooped up the dog and brought her home. The pup was about a year old and looked like she was a terrier/Dalmatian mix (although a DNA test has since indicated that she is primarily a mix of Mexican street dog, Bluetick Coonhound and German Shepherd). Once the rescue team got her cleaned up, spayed, vaccinated and dewormed, she was ready to come to her new home.

Jenna and PJ had bonded so quickly that there was no question she would be a good companion, but Jenna needed more. She wanted PJ to be a service dog, which meant she needed to acquire some specific skills over and above learning to sit and walk well on a leash. So Jenna got down to training her right away. The concentration it required of them gave both PJ and Jenna a positive goal to work toward.

Jenna began by teaching PJ some intervention tactics. People with autism have a kind of sensory processing disorder that causes them to experience neurological overload at times. One expert has described it as a neurological "traffic jam." In these instances, a technique called deep pressure therapy is very useful in calming the person's nervous system and helping them settle down. In 1992, Temple Grandin, a renowned American academic and animal behaviourist who is also a high-functioning autistic person, wrote about how she managed her anxiety by creating a unique "squeeze machine" to calm her jangled nerves. Fifteen minutes of being "hugged" by her machine had a deeply calming effect. The squeeze machine demonstrated the way in which deep pressure can be helpful to people with autism who are unsettled. Hugging helps, as does applying pressure to some parts of the autistic person's body.

Jenna set out to train PJ how to do her own form of DPT by having her sit in Jenna's lap or actually lie on top of Jenna when she's in a supine position. "When I'm getting into panic attacks, if I'm starting to feel that way, if I sit down or lie down and have her do DPT, it will calm me down so significantly that the likelihood is I'm not going to have a panic attack or an anxiety attack. It's like using a weighted blanket—it just makes you feel more secure. And she's like a walking weighted blanket for me."

Some people with autism also do something called "stimming," a repetitive behaviour that helps them deal with overstimulation, fear or excitement. It has a calming effect, but depending on the behaviour, stimming can also be injurious. In Jenna's case, it inflicts damage because she isn't aware of doing it. "It's something that makes you feel comfortable in uncomfortable situations, so a lot of people who are on the autism spectrum play with their fingers or a necklace or they'll play with their hair. I will scratch. It can get really bad, to the point where I will scratch myself completely raw."

Jenna has taught PJ to intervene when she begins scratching. When PJ puts her paws *on top* of Jenna's hand, and slides her nose *under* her hand, it's an alert for Jenna to stop. "She figured out pretty quickly that when I was scratching, it was a cue that she had to do something." The signal diverts Jenna from absent-mindedly hurting herself, especially in overwhelming situations. "Before, I didn't realize that I was doing it until I was in a lot of pain. Now I don't have to worry about that because she gives me a sign that that's what's going on."

Jenna's three years of self-imposed confinement ended almost immediately. Being with PJ has done wonders for Jenna's self-confidence and freed her from her own dark thoughts so that she can leave the house and go into the world, making it possible to go to the dentist, stores and family events. "One of my biggest problems for a long time was putting thoughts into other people's heads and believing that that's what they were thinking." It's taken more than just PJ to help Jenna cope with this tendency, but the dog has been instrumental in opening the world back up for her owner.

And interestingly, there's another reason why Jenna finds the outside more easily understood when she has PJ by her side. Jenna doesn't know how to respond to "small talk." For benign questions like, "Hey, how about this weather?" she doesn't understand how she's supposed to respond. "But I don't really have to worry about small talk when she's with me, because people are more likely to say, 'What a cute dog,' rather than 'the weather's nice.' I have a subject that I am familiar with, so

I don't have to think outside the box. It's all right there. And I can discuss how wonderful my dog is."

It all boils down to this, Jenna says. "It's hard for me to be around people because I feel like I'm always being judged. But with her, there's no judgment. There is no prejudice. All I have to do is look at her and I know I love her. She loves me. And that's all that matters."

Cheyenne

Transcending Trauma

Jason is forty-eight years old: a bearded, six-foot-six gentle giant of a man. He was a firefighter for twenty years, a first responder who faced physical and emotional risks every day of his working life. His dream job damaged him, inflicting hellacious pain and suffering. The result is that he is now fragile, and without two very special dogs, Blaze and Cheyenne, it's almost certain he would not be here and functioning.

Jason was predisposed to a life of service, coming from a family of front-line workers. His father, whom he reveres, is a retired undercover drug squad cop, and his younger brother is a detective. As a teenager, Jason was drawn to a tight group of like-minded friends. "I met these guys and we never talked about being first responders, but, starting at fourteen, the four of us were always together. We always had each other's backs and we protected people that were being picked on. We lost track of each other when we graduated, but interestingly, Ryan became a Toronto firefighter, Blair became a Toronto police officer, and Andrew became an Ottawa police officer."

At eighteen Jason became a volunteer firefighter, and when he was twenty-three he became the youngest person hired on at his fire station. Firefighting wasn't just a job, it was a calling, and he loved his work. "It's a very proud feeling, to work as a firefighter. For me, it was to be of service in any way that I could," he says.

Firefighters are often the first to arrive at the scene of a crisis, and studies have shown that repeated exposure to trauma makes them more likely to become depressed, feel anxiety and have suicidal thoughts. They are also at a higher risk of committing suicide. One study of Montreal firefighters found they "face elevated risks of common mental health issues, with distress rates estimated at around 30 percent, surpassing those of many other occupational groups."

Jason is one of the unlucky 30 percent who develop post-traumatic stress disorder, and his is extreme. He suffers from many complex PTSD symptoms, including debilitating depression and anxiety. "There was a period where I was so depressed that I could sleep till 7 p.m. at night, and I couldn't wait to go back to sleep at 9 p.m."

Experts say that PTSD can be "triggered by a terrifying event—either experiencing it or witnessing it." Jason's PTSD was punched into high gear by one particularly traumatizing residential fire he fought in 2006. Firefighters from two fire stations were on a roof and the situation was becoming unstable. The officers in charge made some decisions that Jason considered unsafe, and Jason spoke up. "I said to my captain, we need to get off this roof. I recognized the roof was getting dangerously soft," he remembers. "When I saw the smoke changing from a light colour to a black colour, I knew that what's next is fire." Suddenly one of his colleagues had a twenty-foot flame in his face. "I went up to him, I grabbed him by the shoulder of his air pack, and I said, 'Let's get the fuck back.' We walked back about five steps, and he fell through the roof. He is a big guy to begin with, but our gear is an extra 100 pounds. So, I was holding 370 pounds in one hand. For some reason, I didn't go through." Two other firefighters stepped in to assist Jason, grabbing him on either side. Somehow, they pulled the man who had fallen through the roof, and themselves, to safety. To this day, Jason is shocked that they survived. "It doesn't even make sense that the four of us didn't fall through together. There's no explanation of why or how we got out of there. And on top of that, being able to hold him and pull him back up, it doesn't even make sense." The shock was one thing. Jason also had to process the fact that four people almost died, in part, he believes, because of poor decision-making by senior officers. On top of that, he was upset that such a dangerous event in his professional life warranted a one-line mention in the local newspaper. All these years later, remembering it causes him to cry, it's still that powerful.

Jason says that in firefighting, as in the military and other front-line work, there is a kind of "tough guys don't cry" mentality. "It's the same toxic masculinity that exists in all these careers to keep going, keep going," he says. "It didn't matter how horrific the call we went to was—whether it involved a baby, a child, whatever it was, the way to deal with it was black humour, making jokes about it. That was the standard for how to deal with traumatic events. It still is today. We're our own worst enemies," he says.

He was thirty-one years old when he fought that fire, and he says that at the time he was too young to understand how to handle the emotional fallout he experienced. "Looking back, I recognize major symptoms were happening. I just didn't know what to do about it. So what I did was I just kept going." After the fire, Jason came home and put on a brave face for his wife. "I didn't have the knowledge I have now to be able to say to her, 'You don't need to know what happened last night, I just need you to hold me.' Instead, what I did was I gave her a kiss and I told her to have a great day at work. I remember her walking out to her car and going off to work, and then I went to my room and cried all day."

Jason says, "I won't ask for help on almost anything, so that's one of my other problems." He was a go-it-alone person, perhaps somewhat like his father, whom Jason describes as his biggest hero. "To this day I'm still teaching my dad that it's okay to hug another man," he says, somewhat ruefully. Jason's marriage wasn't working either, and it eventually ended in a heartbreaking crash.

Jason's life was in shambles, his physical health a mess, and his mental health faltering. "I was in fight-or-flight mode after that incident; my system was jacked right out of control," he says. Adding to his crisis was a serious back injury in 2010 that put him in hospital. He began to unravel. "I started having flashbacks, and I really couldn't differentiate what was real and what wasn't, because a flashback is a daytime dream. It can be extremely real; your physiology can become a part of it, it's not just a memory." The back injury confined him to bed for two and a half months and he lost twenty-five pounds. Although he was told that he might never work as a firefighter again, with sheer grit and determination he regained his strength and was cleared to resume his duties.

In September of 2011 Jason was fighting a residential fire, and while in the attic pulling out insulation so he could get at the fire, Jason's personal protective equipment (PPE) became exposed to cellulose, a fibre insulation. It was frigidly cold that day, and when he and his crew came out of the building, they didn't follow protocol and wash down and decontaminate their PPE, also known as bunker gear, because it was so cold. "When I took off my mask, my bunker gear was covered in insulation, essentially cellulose, and a wind blew and I breathed it in." That led to another round of being in and out of hospital, bouncing between doctors and diagnoses, while getting sicker. On top of the assault on his lungs, his PTSD symptoms were spiralling out of control. When he finally found his way to a lung specialist, the doctor was as concerned about Jason's mental health as he was about his physical situation. "I ended up with a doctor who had been studying firefighters from New York City," he says, "and what he told me was, 'Jason, if we need to get you new lungs, I'm the guy who can do that,' but he said, 'I can't fix your head.' And then I just started bawling my eyes out."

Jason knew that he needed psychiatric care. So did his family. "I just kept getting sicker and more injured." Getting the right help took Herculean effort, with his father pushing hard to get his son the help he needed. Jason was finally admitted to a facility that had a program to treat first responders. "When I arrived, I was supposed to be going into a two-month program called Post-Traumatic Stress Recovery, which sounds really good, on paper, but when they assessed me, I was so sick that they said that I wasn't well enough to be in the stabilization program." What ensued was six months of treatment, some of it very tough, but he made it through and came home to begin rebuilding his life inch by inch.

The idea of getting a therapy dog first came up during sessions with a psychologist who had a Standard Poodle in her office. She suggested he think about getting one for himself. In 2016 he bought a black and white Parti Poodle and called her Blaze. Jason had her assessed as a potential therapy dog, and he was selected to receive the 2016 Elijah Harper Service Dog Award, which was set up by MSAR and George Leonard in memory of the Oji-Cree politician who was the first Aboriginal member of the Legislative Assembly of Manitoba. The award is given to a "deserving member of the public" and comes with financial support and ongoing training. "Blaze was four months old, and they trained me to train her; they sent a trainer to [me] and I would fly to [them] to learn what I needed to learn," he says. Jason and Blaze made quick progress and in no time, Blaze was wearing a service dog vest and looking out for Jason.

Crowds and busy places flustered Jason and would upset his body chemistry. PTSD can cause severe disruptions to the digestive system, and Jason's system would be so rattled by an outing that he'd be housebound for days. It wasn't long before he noticed that Blaze was having a positive impact on these reactions. "After a month of having Blaze, I was not being sick anymore. That was the first thing that I noticed." When Blaze sensed an anxiety attack, she would get between Jason's legs and do deep pressure therapy by pushing up against one of his legs, which calmed his nervous system and helped regulate his emotions. Jason always had a finely tuned ability to anticipate when something was about to happen. "I could drop a knife off the counter, and I could catch it before the floor, by the handle," he says. But having PTSD meant that morphed into an abnormal state of alertness, with heightened startle responses. This made being in any public place uncomfortable. "In a restaurant, if I can't sit against the wall, she will sit behind me and create space."

Hypervigilance puts the body into constant fight-or-flight mode, flooding the body with cortisol, the body's alarm system. Blaze was trained to ensure there was always enough room around Jason that he could relax and tone down his hypervigilant responses.

With great trepidation, Jason agreed in 2017 to participate in a television program about first responders and their dogs, and with Blaze's help he braved a visit to the firehouse he'd been avoiding for years. While he was there, a fellow firefighter told him about a program called Project Trauma Support, which addresses PTSD and moral injury (morally injurious events are said to threaten one's deeply held beliefs and trust) in first responders (police, paramedics, firefighters, corrections officers) and military members/veterans. He enrolled for a six-day residential session. "It not only saved my life, but it gave me a life I never believed was possible, and Blaze was right there alongside me," he remembers. "Part of the treatment was in the bush, and overnight we had a foot of snow. Blaze was off leash doing what she loved, bounding through the snow, and I remember I yelled, 'That's what I want for my life! It's joy, it's pure joy!"

It was one of the first moments of happiness Jason had felt in eons. It was also the moment he remembers deciding to train Blaze as an off-leash-certified service dog, which he undertook. At the end of the training, she did a five-day test that she passed with flying colours; this added another level of freedom to Jason's life. He was able to take her anywhere—into a mall without a leash or into a small store where he could ask her to lie down and she'd stay until he finished shopping. "The connection between a service dog and its handler is psychological, it's emotional. The psychological connection is ongoing, twenty-four hours a day, seven days a week. Vest on, vest off, these animals are working. And they're intervening in whatever way they're going to instinctively, and then whatever way they're trained to."

That connection allowed Jason to begin to rebuild his life. He took on advocacy work, giving dozens of speeches about the importance of service dogs. "While I spoke to thousands of people, she was with me by my side and had my back and took care of me." In 2019, Jason's name came up when Bill C-211, an act to establish a federal framework on PTSD, received royal assent and became law in Canada. Todd Doherty, the member of Parliament who had championed the bill, said of Jason, "When I first met him, I was speaking at a first responder conference with respect to post-traumatic stress disorder and my Bill C-211. Jason was a shell of a man. He could hardly stand up without shaking. PTSD had absolutely racked both his emotional and physical well-being. Sixteen months later, he was given a service dog by the name of Blaze, and Jason was able to come out of his house without being impacted by all that was going on. Blaze absolutely transformed his life."

Jason and Blaze were together for seven years, during which time he made a beeline for the country and began to build a house for himself. "I lived in the [same] area up until four years ago. I had realized for quite some time that I needed more space, just a quieter place to live. I moved to Calabogie, Ontario, about an hour northwest of Ottawa." In September of 2023 he made his last payment on the house, and then tragedy struck again. "The day that I finished this house, I threw Blaze's ball twice in the laneway, and she couldn't find it. It was a Saturday, and at lunch I knew there was something wrong. I rushed her to the emergency vet in Ottawa. I knew it was bad, and they tried to do everything for her." What the vet discovered was that Blaze was riddled with cancer, and Jason had to make the heartbreaking decision to have her put down that evening. "When I lost Blaze, I was so lost," he says, crying, "because that psychological connection you have means that every time you go through a door, like you hold it for a second, right? Well, she wasn't there."

Jason called George Leonard that Saturday night, and two days later the phone rang. George had secured funding to get Jason another dog, whenever he was ready. Telling this part of the story, Jason is completely overcome with emotion. In November 2023, Jason flew to Winnipeg to get another dog especially trained for people with acute PTSD. "When Blaze passed away, he told me there were four possibilities, but he had one in mind, which was Cheyenne. I didn't realize till I got there that she was personally trained by him," he says. "The other trainers would spend time with her because she's so sweet, and more than one of them told me that they never thought George would ever give her up. So I'm pretty lucky."

Cheyenne is a petite black and white Sheepadoodle, and she does look like a miniature clone of Blaze. She is rarely away from Jason's side. Both Blaze and Cheyenne were trained to notice and respond to Jason's anxiety, even when it manifests subtly. While we talk, he pats Cheyenne constantly, and she lies snuggled into his side on the couch. Before he even realizes that he is becoming unsettled by reliving some of the memories, she begins to nudge him gently but insistently, eventually diverting his attention from the subject at hand. Recognizing that his anxiety levels are climbing, Jason takes a break, and they go to the backyard where she runs about. And while he watches her leap through the snow, taking pleasure in her antics, he visibly relaxes.

Diversion is one of her tactics, and making physical contact is another. She will sometimes step up on Jason, licking him while putting her head underneath his arm. Her weight is a kind of pressure therapy. When he is standing, Cheyenne will stand against him, pushing him from the side, leaning into him. "She's letting me know that my anxiety is too high."

Blaze's name was a good fit because of Jason's profession and because she helped him blaze a new trail. "She not only saved my life, she also directed me in ways that allowed me to recover," says Jason. Cheyenne has taken the baton now, which is as important as ever. As Jason says, "If it weren't for these incredible service dogs, I would be six feet under."

Daisy

Affair of the Heart

Life, from the outset, has been profoundly complicated for Keri-Lynn.

She came into the world in 1971 born to a teenage mother. She was a "blue baby," with a congenital heart condition known as transposition of the great arteries (TGA). As Keri-Lynn explains, "A baby is born with their arteries transposed so the aorta and the pulmonary artery are not in the place they should be, like a normal heart. You're very sick because you're not getting oxygen and you have a blue tinge, like my fingernails were blue, my lips were blue." On top of that, she had a toonie-sized hole in her heart.

Her mother had been abandoned by the baby's father during her pregnancy, so she gave Keri-Lynn up at birth—not because she wanted to, but because, at eighteen, she couldn't see her way through. Keri-Lynn was supposed to be adopted, but when the designated family learned of her health issues, they balked.

She was so very fragile that she spent the first weeks of her life alone at the Hospital for Sick Children in Toronto.

When she was two months old, she was put into foster care with an English expatriate family. But even that wasn't easy. When her foster parents wanted to adopt her, they were told they were considered too old to take on a child. They went to court and they won. As Keri-Lynn wryly observes, the court decided that "nobody else wants to adopt this sick baby, she's probably not going to live past the age of four, let's let this family adopt her."

(Twenty-five years later, Keri-Lynn would apply to Children's Aid to see if she could find her birth mother, and in five years she found her—remarkably they were living just twenty minutes away from each other.)

Keri-Lynn outlived expectations, and when she was four years old, she had corrective surgery for the hole in her heart. She flourished, and at her yearly hospital checkups, the results were always good. "I thought I was fixed because my mom and dad were letting me do whatever I wanted," Keri-Lynn says. "Well, not whatever I wanted, but you know what I mean, like a normal kid, you know, climb trees, I did it all. I broke my arm three times doing stupid things. I think because of that, I just lived my life normally."

On the surface, she was a normal kid, even though she was bullied and had few friends, and she still doesn't fully understand why. Still, she made her own fun, and her mother made sure she had horseback riding and dance lessons.

She went into her teenage years as a wild child. She wore the full goth getup—complete with a mohawk and a nose ring—listened to punk rock and frequented goth clubs in Toronto. "Yeah, we had a lot of fun," she remembers.

Keri-Lynn had no inkling she would have trouble with her heart later in life. But unbeknownst to her, it was still working too hard to get enough oxygen pumped into her body, and she was "kind of like an eighteen-wheeler with a Pinto engine."

At twenty-eight, when she became pregnant, Keri-Lynn began to experience arrhythmias. She had no idea carrying a child could be dangerous to her, but when her GP did a pregnancy test and it came back positive, he "tore a strip off" her, Keri-Lynn says. "Oh, he was so angry. 'How could you do this to yourself?' he thundered. And I said, 'Well, I'm keeping the baby because this could be my only chance to have a baby.'" It was a decision that would have the most wonderful outcome—a healthy baby boy born in 1999.

But years later, in 2013, Keri-Lynn's health really began to fail. She'd been wrestling with her mental and physical well-being since her son's birth and hadn't been taking care of herself. She was in rough shape, depressed, smoking and overweight, with high blood pressure. She was sedentary, carrying 186 pounds on a tiny five-foot-two frame. She was also going into heart failure, and her doctor read her the riot act. She listened, and quit smoking, lost a ton of weight and adopted a healthy lifestyle.

In the space of a year, Keri-Lynn became the poster child for turning one's life around. She lost sixty-seven pounds and was running and working out regularly. She looked great. But there was only so much she could do. Her efforts did put the heart failure into remission temporarily, but her heart had an irreversible structural problem. She explains, "As people like me with TGA grow older, our right ventricle starts to fail. It gets enlarged, it gets tired and the scarring [from the original heart operation] can actually cause electrical issues within the heart, and you get arrhythmias."

She is matter-of-fact about where her condition left her. "Because of the way the heart defect is, it'll catch up with you no matter how hard you try to be healthy, right? Your right ventricle is going to fail. You're just kind of screwed that way."

Eventually Keri-Lynn had a pacemaker put in, in 2017, which helped—until it didn't.

Which brings us to Daisy.

Keri-Lynn and her husband, Darren, have always been dog people. She can't remember a time when her family didn't have dogs. In 2018, their much-beloved German Shorthaired Pointer named Woofie died, and they were devastated. Anxious to fill the loss, they began looking for a puppy that resembled the dog they had just lost. When they spotted Daisy in a litter of Lab/German Shepherd/Bernese Mountain Dog puppies, it was love at first sight.

Keri-Lynn felt an instant connection. She says, "[There was] real electricity when I picked her up that first time. I knew she was my dog." They have become inseparable. "She'll sit with me in the kitchen as I cook. She sleeps with me on my bed." And most fortuitously, Daisy stays close to Keri-Lynn while she's working.

On June 15, 2021, it was a regular Tuesday and Keri-Lynn, like so many others during the pandemic, was working from her office at home. She had just finished an intense online meeting with colleagues during which, as she describes it, a work issue had come up that she felt passionate about fixing. So she was feeling some stress, but she was used to that.

When she stood up, she felt a popping in her head. "It sounded like a bunch of bubble wrap going off in my head. I didn't have any pain. But then I must have fainted, because I collapsed and I found myself on the floor. I couldn't move my left side, so I couldn't get up. I tried, but I couldn't."

Keri-Lynn drifted in and out of consciousness, but she does remember Daisy standing over her, licking her face. "I was close to the wall, and I could move my right side, so I was kicking the wall to try and get Darren's attention." To no avail.

She remembers calling for help, but her words were garbled and Darren, who is a shift worker, was upstairs, sound asleep. Daisy ran up to their bedroom, jumped on the bed, licked Darren, jumped off the bed, back on the bed, off the bed, until she woke him up.

Darren headed downstairs toward the back door, following the dog, wondering why Keri-Lynn hadn't let the dog out to do her business. Daisy ran ahead and led him down to Keri-Lynn's office in the basement, where Darren found her on the floor, collapsed. He could see her face was drooping and, realizing that she had had a stroke, called 911.

What had happened? The doctors told her she had had an arrhythmia that wasn't intercepted by her pacemaker. That led to a blood clot in her heart, which shot to her head and caused a stroke.

Throughout the entire ordeal, other than fetching Darren, Daisy never left Keri-Lynn's side.

If she hadn't gone to get Darren? Keri-Lynn was told that if the dog hadn't gone to get help, and Darren had continued to sleep, unaware of the situation, "it would have been too late to do anything." She could have been profoundly compromised or died.

But because Daisy alerted Darren *and* they got help within an hour, *and* the ambulance took Keri-Lynn to a hospital that specializes in handling strokes, *and* a doctor was able to take out the clot very quickly, she emerged unscathed by the stroke.

For that, she feels that Daisy is her guardian angel and her protector.

Then, in 2022, Keri-Lynn had more health difficulties. She had a run of ventricular tachycardia, a fast and abnormal heart rhythm (arrhythmia). Each time her pacemaker shocked her back into normal rhythm, but her heart continued to become enlarged and the bouts of arrhythmia were constant. Recurring episodes of arrhythmia can be dangerous, and if an episode lasts for more than a few seconds at a time, it can become life-threatening, causing all heart activity to stop.

Keri's heart was so unstable that any expression of emotion—any kind of happiness or excitement, even eating—would cause pulmonary edema, excessive fluid accumulation in the lungs. Eventually, after a number of trips to the hospital emergency room, her doctors decided it was time for a heart transplant. They admitted her to hospital on January 17, 2023, and listed her for a new heart on March 1, 2023.

However, her doctor was worried that Keri-Lynn wasn't well enough to survive having a transplant. "And so the doctor [said], 'I think we've missed the window of opportunity. I'm going to have put you on a DNR [do not resuscitate order].' That was really scary." But the gods were looking out for Keri-Lynn this time. "Luckily, a week after she said that, a heart came available. And they decided that they would move forward with the transplant."

Two years after the stroke that very easily could have killed her, Keri-Lynn is facing a much rosier future. She has a new heart and she feels like a different person. The physical training she has been doing to get back in shape has paid off in dividends. Just weeks after the transplant, she was out for a five-kilometre hike.

Keri-Lynn has two dogs now. She and Darren got Otis, a German Shorthaired Pointer/Australian Shepherd cross, to keep Daisy company while Keri-Lynn was in and out of hospital before and after her transplant. He's a handful, but the dogs have bonded well. Every day, when Keri-Lynn takes the dogs out for their daily walk, they're getting their exercise, as is she, and that continues to help her on the road to a full recovery.

Lambchop

Sorrow's Soulmate

Lambchop, Alex's Pit Bull Terrier, was the size of a potato when she arrived on the doorstep. She was six weeks old, and she was delivered to Alex by the breeder—a trucker from up around Hudson's Bay. It was kind of a drive-by delivery. On a day in June 2019, he rolled up and handed the pup out the window of his truck.

It was instant love between Alex and the dog she describes as exactly the dog she'd hoped for, "a super ridiculous love machine."

Actually, she was smitten long before this puppy came to her. One of her office mates had a sibling of this little dog, Nellie, who used to come into the office all the time, and Alex fell for her hard. When she heard there was to be a new litter of pups, it was a no-brainer. She had to have one.

Alex is in her forties, a slender blonde with relaxed good looks and a hip, downtown elegance that suits her life in real estate. She's well-educated, gracious, worldly, and very busy with a well-connected clientele. She had to have a dog that could be social with an array of different people.

She'd sought the advice of several trusted veterinarians, asking them, "Listen, am I crazy? I am thinking about getting this dog." Two told Alex, "These dogs are horribly misunderstood," adding that they are "often the best dogs" in the clinic. Another said she'd recently tried to adopt one of her own.

Her own fears about the breed's nature assuaged, Alex set out to bring her parents onside. But instant love wasn't what Alex's family felt. When she told them about her plan, Alex says they "had a heart attack" and were having none of it. Her parents warned that the dog would be banned from the family cottage and kept away from the grandchildren, even though their family had over the years had German Shepherds, a breed that has also been feared as aggressive.

They were afraid that a Pit Bull would be genetically predisposed to violence. Alex kept insisting they had to wait before passing judgment, saying that dogs, like people, respond to their environment and their upbringing, and in the case of a dog, to their training. "I said to my parents, you have to at least meet this dog before you make up your mind."

As soon as Lambchop arrived, they met the tiny puppy, who at that point was small enough to fit into one hand. Lambchop had "giant dumbo bat ears," unlike most of her breed, whose ears are folded flat. Her colouring is a rich mix of velvety brown, charcoal black and grey, and according to Alex, "she has dark, soulful seal eyes, making her look like . . . a baby hippopotamus mixed with a seal, mixed with a manatee."

Mindful that her dog would have to have excellent manners and almost perfect behaviour, Alex was meticulous about training Lambchop, and slowly but surely her family began to come around and accept her.

Three years later, Lambchop would prove to be a godsend to Alex *and* her mother.

Tuesday, April 5, 2022, began as a beautiful spring day. Alex was at her office that morning. It was a particularly busy workday and she had a million things on the go. She'd just come out of a staff meeting when her phone rang. Normally she might have let it ring through to voice mail, but she saw it was her mother, Ardyth, and she answered. "I picked up the phone and my mom was hysterical on the phone, like, 'Your dad's been taken to the hospital, he was hit, he's in a life-threatening condition. You have to come right now!'"

Her seventy-eight-year-old father, Boris Brott, the internationally renowned Canadian orchestral conductor, had been walking to a nearby doctor's appointment not far from his home in Hamilton.

At 10:20 a.m. he was struck down by a hit-and-run driver, a young man with a history of mental health issues and convictions for dangerous and impaired driving.

Alex was frozen. The dog was safe with the dog walker, and Alex managed to get into her car and head for Hamilton. On the way, she frantically called her brothers, people in her parents' lives, anyone who might have some information about her father. "At some point, I spoke to somebody who is a really close friend of ours, and I said something like, 'Okay, well, I'm on my way. Does anyone know if he's out of surgery? Like, what's happening?' And the friend said, 'When was the last time you talked to your mom?' And I was like, 'Fuck.' I hung up the phone and I called my mom back. And of course, she told me to pull over. I just was like, 'No, this just can't even be real.' It still feels so surreal."

Boris Brott had succumbed to his injuries. "My dad was hit by a madman who was on a tear," Alex says. Even though he had previous convictions, "he'd never killed anyone, and he killed my dad. Right outside of my parents' house, a block away. This man hit him and kept driving."

The next days were a blur. She moved into her parents' house to be with her mother. Somebody brought Lambchop out to Hamilton for her.

The family was in complete shock. They have always been extraordinarily close, speaking to each other daily and sharing a family dinner weekly. Alex tells a story about one of her father's romantic gestures toward her mother, her sisters-in-law, and herself. "My dad loved opera, so he had a lot of access to very cool performers and singers. He would pick a song for us and he would have the singer call us on the morning of Valentine's Day and sing us an aria. And it was beautiful."

One year Alex was out with a client when her phone rang. "I said, 'Do you want to hear something cool?'" Alex put the phone on speaker and she and her client listened together. That year her father had invited a man to record the Valentine's offering, and it was gorgeous. Alex remembers that she and her client, a film director, were both blown away.

These messages from her father were the kind of gift that would make any person's heart do a little flip. The last time Alex received one of these audio missives, it was of momentous importance. "Just crazily, last year, my dad decided to sing the aria to us. I have it," she remembers. "He recorded it and texted that to us that morning." She has kept the recording, an enduring if painfully poignant reminder of her father. "I can't listen to it, but I'm so happy I have it."

Alex and Lambchop moved home to Hamilton for a while, but her style of handling her dog was a little at odds with her family's. She'd grown up with "no dogs on the bed or furniture," a rule that hadn't migrated to Alex's house. In those early days, Alex's mum was waking with panic attacks, so she and Alex slept in the same bed. Lambchop was determined to take her place sleeping beside Alex, who remembers, "My mom was really not very cool with it—*at first*." Lambchop prevailed. Alex believes it was as if the dog said, "Nope, actually, my place is right here." Over time she became a constant source of "soft love" next to them, helping them endure the worst moments.

There was reaction from all over the world when the maestro died so shockingly—for months there were memorials and special concerts in his honour—all of which were appreciated but also added to the stress felt by the family, who were just trying to hold each other up. Alex can't imagine not having her dog through those first few months. "That unspoken but very communicative language is something that allows you to get to the next minute . . . and the next hour and . . ." For Alex, Lambchop was, and is, an ongoing reminder, "that you're going to be okay somehow," and she gets tremendous reassurance from the dog's ability to convey, "I'm not asking you anything. I don't need to talk about it with you. I just want to be here with you and sit with you."

It's challenging, to say the least, to come to grips with the death of a loved one, especially under such violent circumstances. Alex says she felt as if someone had torn all the insides out of her body, leaving her exhausted and emotionally barren, like there is nothing left inside. Friends advised her to get therapy, which she did and does. But while therapy is useful, it doesn't leave her feeling healed. "I never come out of it being like, 'Oh, this is so much better.'" However, the comfort she gets from Lambchop is in another league. "After lying on my couch with my dog for an hour, I feel better. So if I could choose which therapy to have, I would pick the dog every day . . . the touch of them, the physical presence of them on you, leaning all of their weight on you, putting their little face in your hand while you're sitting there, like, 'I just want to let you know I love you. I'm right here for you.'"

Serenity

Seizure Safeguard

There are times when support dogs do as much for an entire family as they do for their primary owner. In this family's case, this was definitely true.

When Aidan was fourteen years old, he was bedevilled by a mysterious condition. Without warning he would freeze in his tracks, lose consciousness as if he were asleep, and become completely unresponsive. These episodes would last for minutes at a time, leaving him dazed and unaware of what had happened.

Aidan's parents, David and Julia, first began to sense something was off with their son when he was in ninth grade. It started at Aidan's bedtime. "He would brush his teeth, and normally, we'd see him go by in the hallway," David says. There were evenings when they weren't seeing him walk to his bedroom, and when they checked on him, they'd find him standing stock-still in the hall, eyes closed.

The situation kept getting worse and the episodes were more frequent. "At first they were very short spells," his father remembers. "We would find him passed out in his room at night, or he'd have fallen down the steps." The spells became progressively longer, and sometimes he would be out for fifteen, twenty or thirty minutes.

This continued for three years, with the family calling 911 dozens of times and seeking the advice of numerous doctors. Aidan was in and out of hospital repeatedly. Eventually one neurologist speculated that he could be having seizures, but nobody knew for sure and no one seemed to know why they were happening. Nor did they know how to deal with the seizures when they happened.

It was frightening; Aidan could collapse anywhere. On one family trip, Aidan actually stopped breathing during a spell in their hotel room. Other times he would hyperventilate. "He'd be breathing fine and then all of a sudden he would be breathing really fast," David remembers, "and then he would stop breathing. At that point, he was unconscious."

He and his family began to improvise. They had some paper lunch bags and discovered that if they put them over Aidan's mouth when he was rapid-breathing, "eventually he would come back to normal." But, David says, it didn't always work. "Sometimes he would stop breathing completely for a couple of minutes. It was really, really scary. The hardest part was our son was passing out and we were not getting any answers."

When Aidan was in twelfth grade, he had a series of spells, each one lasting over an hour. A visit to the hospital brought no answers, and the doctors were ready to send him home again. Julia, however, insisted that Aidan be moved to a hospital where doctors could do more testing. The hospital agreed, and with further examination, including video EEG monitoring, doctors realized what was going on in his brain. As David explains, "They wanted to capture one of these events while it was happening. So they put electrode leads on his head, and the doctor asked him to talk about what had been going on at school. And as soon as he started talking, he almost immediately passed out." It was March 4, 2019, and this time, doctors had a diagnosis.

Aidan was having "pseudoseizures," which can appear to be epileptic but are actually caused by trauma or other psychological factors, like stress. One doctor used a computer metaphor to explain what was happening, saying it was as if Aidan's brain had to shut down, take a break and reboot itself.

This was a double revelation to everyone in the family. Now they understood that stress was the cause of the onset of Aidan's symptoms and that he was being bullied at school, a problem he'd concealed from his family and was handling on his own. "He didn't want to talk about it, and he kept it pretty private until the day he opened up to the doctor," says David.

But there was more. "It was not only the stress from bullying. That was the main thing, but Aidan also had received a significant injury where he dislocated his right knee." If Aidan's knee was sore, or if he bumped it, or if he was just in pain, the pain would cause him to have one of these seizures, according to David. They would eventually learn that Aidan's seizures were being caused by panic, stress, anxiety, extreme pain and/or extreme heat.

It's a miracle that Aidan didn't sustain serious injuries during these spells. His parents would hear him falling down the stairs at two or three in the morning. The constant worry was felt by everyone. Aidan's little sister, Deana, would become distraught about the seizures. Julia became hyperprotective of him, especially if he collapsed somewhere public. For David, there was an unexpected consequence, which he remembers with a sheepish smile. "I found that I was a binge eater. I used to go in and raid the fridge, especially before he was diagnosed in 2019, because we didn't know what the heck was going on."

As they began to dig deeper into what was going on at school, Julia and David found that Aidan wasn't getting a lot of support about the bullying, and it was obviously getting to their son in a big way. He was having seizures almost daily. "The sad part of the whole bullying thing was that Aidan had to finish his grade 12 online," David says. Julia interjects with some bitterness that Aidan didn't go to his graduation, either. "We had a personal graduation ceremony in the office with just the family, but none of his friends were there. So there's a lot of sour feelings, at least for me."

A German Shorthaired Pointer named Salut provided the first clue about how to stabilize Aidan's health. Amy, one of Julia's friends, is a breeder who specializes in support dogs. She was with Aidan when he had a spell, and Salut, an eight-month-old puppy of hers, was present when Aidan had another seizure in the hospital. Salut was actually in training to become a cardiac support dog, but without any prompting, he jumped up on the bed and put his paws on Aidan's shoulders, positioning himself so that his weight was on Aidan's chest and belly. This puppy, serendipitously, had the innate ability to sense seizures, a gift only some dogs have. Even without any training, Salut had, in effect, done deep pressure therapy, relaxing Aidan and easing him out of the seizure.

This was a giant clue for Aidan's family. They decided to get him a support dog. In March 2020, one of Amy's dogs had puppies. Matching dogs with their owners is a tricky business, kind of like online dating. A match might look good on paper, but until the two are in the same room together, there's no way of knowing if they're a good fit. This was true here. Amy identified two of her puppies that might suit Aidan's needs. Joy, the one that Amy had in mind, wanted nothing to do with Aidan. But Serenity, the other one, went right over to him, curled up in his lap, and fell asleep.

So it was Serenity, referred to as "Ren" by the family, who came home with them when she was just a puppy. Serenity is a German Shorthaired Pointer. She's leggy and lean, with a cropped tail, short black hair and speckles of white on her chest. Her dark brown almond-shaped eyes give her the look of an old soul.

She demonstrated her value almost immediately. "When she was eight weeks of age," Julia says, "Aidan had one of his seizures. Because Ren was so tiny, and still learning, I walked her over to him and she did the rest. She curled up on his chest and she started to lick his face." Aidan began to come round. David says he had been somewhat skeptical about what a dog might do for Aidan, but seeing is believing. "Even from the first day when Serenity came into our lives and Aidan was there on the floor, it's like the dog was a miracle worker. It just blew my mind. It was like, wow, these dogs do really amazing things."

Serenity's temperament also suits her well for the task. "She's a very calm dog, like you don't even know she's here. She doesn't bark. She just looks out the window and watches the world go by as if she could care less, because she knows what her job is. She's not a guard dog. She's a working dog. And whether she has her harness on or her vest, or even here at home when she doesn't have it on, she knows she's on duty 24/7. She sleeps with Aidan every night." In the event of a nocturnal seizure, Serenity can turn the doorknob and open his bedroom door, run up to the main floor, open a cat gate en route, and make her way to Julia and David's room to alert them.

When Serenity is trying to soothe Aidan during a seizure, she'll crawl up beside him and press her body against his side. "Or she stands over him," Julia says, "and she licks his lips. His teeth are almost clenched, and she manages to get his lips parted and his jaw to open up. And then she licks inside his mouth, almost like she's giving him CPR."

While this might sound unusual, in Aidan's case, it is part of what helps him come around. According to Stanley Coren, a Canadian expert on human-canine interactions, "There is a class of service dog called a 'seizure response dog' which has been trained to assist people when they have a seizure. Their job is to bark or otherwise alert caretakers when an individual has a seizure. Some dogs learn to lie next to someone having a seizure to prevent injury, often licking their faces to try to stimulate them back into consciousness." The remarkable thing about Serenity is that she knew how to do all these things without having to be taught.

Aidan takes Serenity with him pretty well everywhere he goes, and he's able to leave the house with a new-found sense of security. He's doing things he never would have done before, like volunteering for a local Junior B hockey team. But there are still things that are almost guaranteed to bring on a spell. For instance, Aidan is nervous about needles, and when he had a COVID vaccination, his parents warned the nurses that he might pass out. He did, while sitting in a chair, and when paramedics got him onto a gurney, Ren jumped up and stood over Aidan, licking his face and even in his mouth, until he came to.

There's no question Aidan has had fewer seizures since Serenity's arrival. David says Aidan rarely has them now, maybe once a month, because "stress doesn't bother him anymore when Ren is helping him." "When I first started, I didn't know what was going on," says Aidan, "but now that we've got them under control, everything's been better."

Aidan is a man of few words, but he jokes about Serenity's place in the family. "She doesn't like to listen to me when my mom's around in the house, but when we go out, she listens to me." About his own experience with his canine companion, he says simply, "It's been somethin'!"

Princely Presence

One September afternoon in 2016, Ania was walking her dog along a busy downtown thoroughfare when she spotted a tiny animal running toward her along the opposite side of the road. At first sight she thought it might be a fox, but as it got closer, she realized it was a small dog that looked like a scruffy cartoon character with tangled hair, big ears and a long tail. There was no owner in sight. "I could see it coming from two blocks away, ears down, tail flying, running toward downtown, and I thought, 'Wow, this dog is going to die, he's going to get hit by a car, he's not stopping, he's not slowing down.' I couldn't get across the street in front of him because of all the cars, so I took my dog Kasha and started running in the same direction as this little dog was running until the cars started to clear. I cut across the road diagonally, and he was just ahead of me, but somehow he saw, or felt, that I had a dog and he turned around."

The dogs paused to check each other out, giving Ania time to unclip her purse strap and attach it to a thin collar around the little dog's neck. She headed for home with the two dogs beside her, feeling a bit stunned that she had impulsively taken possession of such an odd-looking creature. But she could see that he was in need of some care and attention. "When I got to the front door, I put my own dog inside and looked down at him and realized that he was crawling with fleas," she says. Ania and her boyfriend set up a washing station in her backyard and bathed the foundling. With each rinse, the wash basin swam with dead fleas.

Ania began scanning her neighbourhood, looking for any signs posted about a lost dog, but nothing turned up. Ania didn't plan on having another dog, but she didn't want to give "Fox" up, either. She took the dog to the vet, where she found he was riddled with worms, had an eye infection and hadn't been neutered. The vet estimated he was somewhere between four and five years old, and in remarkably good shape for a dog that had been living rough. Given the way the little dog had been neglected, the vet advised that, if it were up to her, she wouldn't look too hard for his previous owners. Ania took the vet's advice. "Fox was not just a stray; he was a gift for me, and I think I was a gift for him. I still feel that way, profoundly," she says.

Ania had chosen to name the little dog Fox because she thought he looked like a fox, but also because of a novel she had written about Antoine de Saint-Exupéry, the famed French aviator. "The last thing that I had published and was still talking about and thinking about was in large part about Saint-Exupéry writing *The Little Prince*." *The Little Prince* is known for words of wisdom; some of the most profound aphorisms come from a fox that befriends the title character. "The fox tells him that when you tame something you are responsible for it; when you tame a wild thing and get it to trust you, then you must take care of that creature," Ania says, still with a sense of wonder in her voice. "How could I be living with so many of my thoughts revolving around the words of the fox and now have a fox? I had to name him Fox. It was an incredible thing."

Fox was diminutive, with red and white markings, white ankles and legs, black button eyes, and a pear-shaped face with a long pointy nose. Ania had no idea what kind of dog he was. "Some people think he looks like a terrier. Some people think he's part Chihuahua because he's small," she says, "but in doing my research, I came across some pictures of dogs that look extraordinarily like him. They come in three sizes and are called Podengo, the national dog of Portugal. So, he would be the smallest—the Podengo Pequeno." While she couldn't be 100 percent sure of Fox's breed, he certainly displays qualities common to Podengos: he runs like the wind, loves to hunt, is an excellent mouser and rat catcher, and is so fleet of foot he can catch a bat in mid-air.

From day one, the guiding principle that you become responsible forever for what you've tamed, shared by the fox in *The Little Prince*, informed Ania's understanding of her relationship with her little dog. There was a serendipity to the timing of Fox's rescue. He needed a new home, and Ania needed companionship because her own life was in a state of flux.

"At the time that Fox came into my life, I was in the early stages of my first significant relationship post-divorce," she says, "and I was really wanting to make things work with this guy, Frank." What Ania didn't see for quite a long time was his drinking habit, because he didn't talk about it. By the time Ania twigged to what was going on in her relationship with Frank, she had already fallen in love with him. He was a good guy, but his drinking brought chaos into their relationship, and he and Ania became embroiled in messy, complicated codependency.

On the upside, Frank had a big heart and was a dog lover. He had a Greyhound rescue he adored, and when Fox came along six months into his relationship with Ania, he fell hard for Fox too, a feeling reciprocated by Fox. Also in the mix was Kasha, half Miniature Poodle and half Wheaten Terrier, and such a sweet animal that they called her Saint Kasha when she passed away. The dogs became surrogate children to him, Ania says. On the downside, Frank had come from a traumatic background, and his way of coping with the fallout from his tough beginnings was binge drinking. Ania had survived an alcoholic father, and when Frank's behaviour began to mirror her father's, it was a miserable reminder of a too-familiar cycle of hurt, disappointment, abject apologies and promises that things would get better. The dogs were not impervious to the tensions. "Fox knew what was going on, he knew when I was hurting, and if it was loud, if there was yelling, he was sensitive to that too," Ania says. "It was a really hard time of life and Fox was in the midst of all that. Frank's dog was a lovely, lovely dog, but he wasn't sensitive the way that Fox was. He would just put his head down and sleep, while Fox would be watching with his little eyes and ears moving," she remembers.

Fox and Ania became a dyad of refuge when things were going off the rails with Frank. Although Fox wasn't trained as a support dog, he intuited Ania's need to be shored up. "Fox is the sort of dog that will come up and stand on you and lick away your tears. If I would so much as sniffle, if I was crying, he would come over to see if he had to make me feel better. He did a lot of work. He got a lot of love, too, but there's no question that he was tied up in the emotion of things," she says. Ania didn't know about deep pressure therapy, or realize that when Fox stood on her, the pressure of his paws on her body could have the effect of calming her central nervous system. She did, however, recognize that physical contact with him had a positive impact on her sense of well-being. "The touch of a dog's paw is one of the incredible things in life. Even if they've just put their paw on your arm or your leg, there's something about it that is unlike anything else. There's something special."

Ania held out hope that things between Frank and herself would improve. "I really believed that if Frank understood how worthy he was of love he could follow through on the work that would help him to heal." But he didn't heal and continued to drink. Meanwhile, Ania hid the truth about what was happening in their relationship from everyone around her. "I wasn't telling my mom or my siblings or friends what I was going through. It was shameful . . . because I knew better," she says. "My world was getting smaller, as it does when you are very wrapped up with somebody in a codependent relationship."

Things became untenable after Ania loaned her car to Frank and it wound up damaged in a crash. Over the next months it was not uncommon for her to find him drunk and passed out. In 2020, she finally called an end to the tumultuous relationship. She was heartbroken, but through it all, Fox was by her side. "He was always steady, always loving," she says.

The breakup happened at the beginning of the COVID-19 pandemic. Ania was alone in a new place and was geographically disconnected from her family, who lived south of the border. She was brought low by a deep depression. "I was very isolated. I wasn't reaching out to people, but again, I had Fox. I would walk Fox. A lot of times I was crying when I was walking Fox, but I was walking him," she says, remembering times when she was almost phobic about leaving her house. "Before Fox, it was not unusual for me to stand at the door and try and try to convince myself to go out and not be able to do it. Having Fox broke that."

Ania and Fox began taking long walks along a local river, finding pleasure in being in nature. Ania credits these days spent out-of-doors with nurturing a shift in how she saw herself. She was becoming a different, more spiritual person. It wasn't something she was doing alone, however. It was the company of her little dog that facilitated the transition. "I've had Fox a long time now. Every day and every night I thank him for coming, and I thank the universe for giving him to me."

Looking back, Ania has done a lot of healing in the nine years she and Fox have been together. She's grateful every single day. But now he's aging, and she has to prepare herself for a day when he will no longer be by her side. "I know he's getting old now. You really would never know it most of the time, but for a long time I have been preparing myself for him to leave because it's going to be very, very difficult. But I know that if I can hold on to that higher sense of the miracle of him coming to me for a reason other than that I needed a dog, or that he needed help, then when he leaves, I will be able to hold on to the gratitude that this incredible spirit came to be with me for that time. And I want him to know every single day that he's done so much good."

There is a poetic spirit in the way Ania speaks to Fox about the process of aging. "I tell him, 'Whenever you are ready, whenever you've completed what you came here to do, I want you to know that I'm letting you go with incredible gratitude. You did beautiful work here. You are a beautiful, loving angel.'"

Cheryl

Renewed Horizons

"I don't know what happened, I tripped over something on the sidewalk, I was holding two briefcases and I couldn't catch myself. I think it was that accident and flying home with two black eyes that prompted me to start investigating guide dogs." Anne did that face-plant in 2010, while she was in Ottawa for a conference. She was in her early fifties and had been coping with declining eyesight for most of her life, but this was a tipping point.

Anne was born and raised in St. John's, Newfoundland. She is the oldest of eight children and was born with a genetic condition, a degenerative myopia that caused her to be extremely nearsighted. Her nearsightedness became evident when she was five or six months of age, and when she was learning to crawl, she would go feel her way around the perimeter of the room. She remembers, "If I wanted to look at something, I would hold it very, very close to my face." She had been outfitted with glasses before she was two, and as a youngster wore what she describes as "really thick goggly things" with a band that went around the back of her head to keep them on her face. Every year, Anne needed a new prescription; her glasses got to be so thick that they would fall right off whenever she lowered her head. "My childhood was a little on the bumpy side. On the playground, whenever anybody shouted Helen Keller, I knew they meant me," she recalled.

When she was twelve years old, Anne was prescribed contact lenses. It was 1969, and they were much too costly for most people. "I do remember they were incredibly expensive and had to be insured. It was a big deal! But the big deal for me was going back to school without those glasses, and it completely changed my school experience." She was still very nearsighted, but she no longer stood out as different. She learned to "pass" as sighted. Her social life improved, but some of her academics suffered because she couldn't see what was on the blackboard. "Some subjects, depending on your aptitude in that subject, really do require blackboard instruction. Algebra still makes no sense to me," she says. "I never passed a math test after grade 9, so I never graduated high school, which has cast a pall over my entire life."

When she got out into the working world, Anne learned by doing. She gravitated toward employment she felt confident she could do, where, she jokes, she didn't have to measure anything or use heavy machinery. Anne is a personable woman, a self-described extrovert, and she flourished in jobs that needed service and communication skills, like waitressing. She was able to do that until she had children, when shiftwork in the service industry didn't fit anymore.

However, because she was so adept at covering up her visual limitations, she later landed a job as an archivist with a local visual arts organization, and what began as a temporary gig evolved into full-time work there. "Within three years I was executive director of the organization," she says, "and remained in that position until I had a really cataclysmic sudden reduction in vision."

The cataclysm happened one summer night in 2005. She remembers it vividly, right down to the novel she was reading. She had finished *One Hundred Years of Solitude* and gone to sleep. When she woke, her vision was unusually clouded. "I thought I couldn't get the steam off my bathroom mirror. I was trying to put makeup on, and I couldn't see myself in the mirror, and I couldn't figure out why the fan wasn't getting rid of the steam," she remembers. On her way to work she still couldn't bring things into focus. She could see forms, but nothing more. She describes the experience as seeing a "psychedelic swirl of optical confetti." Anne kept working, hoping things would settle down and she'd regain what vision she'd had. "I tried to do what I'd been doing my whole life, which was just go to work and pass as sighted," she remembers. "I think it might have just been critical mass that my retina was so fragile from multiple minihemorrhages, which are not painful or visible, they just occur. Maybe another minihemorrhage happened, but it knocked out the vision that I really needed and won't be able to reclaim." She found this period emotionally hard, like it was something she "had to hide and keep a secret."

Anne struggled to manage her job, but after a few months gave in and resigned, conceding the change in her eyes was permanent. "I couldn't read quickly enough, even with accommodations. I thought my ability to read things with the same speed and ease as sighted people would return, like I would adapt again, but that didn't happen, and I think I grieved deeply for about two years." It was a psychosocial journey as well. "There was a lot to learn, to absorb and to adjust to inside myself. And at that time, I really didn't know my rights as a disabled employee."

St. John's is where Anne was born and raised and where she has deep roots, professionally and personally. It's a robust place with a dynamic arts scene. "It's like living in a very big, small town," Anne says. "Everybody knows everybody, and everybody knows *about* everybody. There are three or four pubs where everybody hangs out. You can walk into one of those pubs any evening of the week, and there's going to be somebody there that you know, you're not going to be alone, drinking your pint or whatever." Although no one excluded Anne, this latest diminishment of her vision had an inhibiting effect on her. She describes herself as the kind of person who would once enter a room, hail a friend or acquaintance, and make her way over to see them. But when she could no longer see who was there, going into a public space became daunting. "How do you go into a room with people who have known you for years and years but never known anything about this because you haven't talked about it, which I hadn't, and then, all of a sudden, sit them down and tell them you're going blind. I mean, the script, please? How awkward or what?" Her social life shrank and she became depressed.

The whole of Anne's life seemed to be in a tumbler. She reflects on it with some humour now, but it was a difficult and intense period of her life. "The marriage collapsed. The kids left home. My sight crashed," she says, with a rueful laugh. Anne describes the years 2007 to mid-2010 as a blur of emotional pain. She crammed her days with keeping busy for the sake of avoiding what was happening to her. "I remember picking up *Reader's Digest*, when they still existed in doctors' offices, and there was an article, "The Ten Most Stressful Life Events" or something. I'm sitting there, as depressed as Lady Macbeth, and I'm going, tick, tick, tick. It was that kind of time, but it was also during that time that I started investigating guide dogs," she says.

After the humiliating fall Anne had taken in Ottawa, getting a guide dog was becoming a matter of protecting her own safety. She applied to a guide dog school, and in relatively short order, she was approved and put on a waiting list. A year later, in 2011, a trainer from the school flew to St. John's to meet Anne. She arrived bearing an empty harness. It was a training exercise—and perhaps a test to see how well suited Anne would be to handle the special relationship with a guide dog. "We went for a walk, and I held the handle of the harness, and she held the dog end of the harness." It must have been a funny scene, Anne walking behind a human pretending to be leading her like a dog. The trainer asked her to follow the signals she sent her through the harness. "It's amazing how much information you get just holding the handle, and within five minutes of walking and not having to look down at the ground to make sure I wasn't going to trip over something, I felt free. I knew, immediately, this was the right thing for me."

This kind of training prepped Anne well for making her way around a city of many hills and complicated, winding streets. About six months later, Anne was matched with a dog. She was invited to the school where she would meet her new canine companion. "There were three other people in my class, each of us from a different part of the country." Anne loved the whole process. "It's like summer camp for grown-ups, and you get to leave with a dog!" She and her classmates did some preliminary training together for three days, after which they were introduced to their dogs. "I was sitting there, my heart pumping, and I couldn't wait to see this dog.

"The knock came on the door, the door opened, and this glossy little Black Lab pranced in, walked up to me, and laid her head on my lap, and we were pretty much inseparable for the next twelve years. That was my dog, Cheryl," Anne remembers, grinning. "It's one of the best things that ever happened to me, getting my first guide dog. It completely changed my view of what was possible for me."

Anne and Cheryl flew home together from Ottawa. It was a long trip, made longer by some delays, but Anne found it all very exciting. "For the first time, I didn't feel self-conscious about sight loss, and I was strutting it through that airport. There I was, with this gorgeous black dog, by myself, doing something that people didn't expect to see me do or expect to see any person with a disability do, like drag suitcases and a dog around an airport at three in the morning unassisted. I kind of take subversive pleasure in that," she says. "It was a very windy night, we got stuck in an airport for hours longer than we should have, so there were two airports and a lot of people, and I just felt so proud and so, 'Look at me!' I hadn't felt that way in a long time, and it never went away. It was transformative."

Like any love affair, the initial thrill gave way to the demands of real life, and Anne and Cheryl had some serious adjusting to do. Anne knew every nook and cranny of the old city, right down to cracks in the sidewalks, but Cheryl had to become familiar with them too. There were also newer streets that were unfamiliar to Anne, and the city was becoming busier than ever. "We have a chaotic traffic situation here, with very narrow streets on steep hills in a province where it seems like everybody wants the biggest SUV they can find, and we also have turbulent weather. The wind always blows in St. John's, there's often a lot of precipitation with that wind, and it's a challenging environment. And in the winter a very small percentage of sidewalks get cleared. It's sadly normal for pedestrians to be walking in moving traffic along with drivers, because there's nowhere else to go. I can't do that with a guide dog."

There was some urgency to getting Cheryl settled. When a guide dog is brought into a new environment, they need time—sometime months—to become familiar with the smells and sounds and sights of their surroundings. While they're getting to know their new owner. If all this doesn't happen successfully, a guide dog's training can be jeopardized. They had returned in November, which hadn't given Anne much time to familiarize herself and the dog to the city before the fall of snow caused a problem.

Over and above that, Anne had her own personal challenge. "What I perceived as the social benefits of having a dog were probably more critical to me than how the actual mobility piece works," she says. "Nobody knew it, but I was about to be making my debut as a person living with a significant sensory issue." Anne was finally ready to let the world in on her secret, but she didn't want it to be a heavy experience. It was especially important to her since she had pulled herself out of depression and wanted to keep that process as light as possible. She wanted to telegraph to people that she was approachable, and she hoped that having a dog would do that.

It didn't always work. Anne uses the phrase "toxic compassion" to describe the reaction she sometimes gets from people when they learn of her disability. She remembers one encounter well. "I ran into a friend of mine who is an artist, and he looked at me and he looked at the dog, and he went, 'What's that on your dog?' She had a reflective sleeve on one of the straps of her harness that said Canadian Guide Dogs for the Blind. So I just said, 'Well, my vision's gotten really bad over the last little while and this is my guide dog.'" The encounter with her friend took place just after the Boston Marathon bombing in April 2013, where three people were killed and hundreds injured. When her friend exclaimed, "Oh, no. That's horrible," Anne found herself on the defensive, saying, "This is not so horrible. But I tell you what is: getting your legs blown off at the end of a marathon." It was a blistering pushback on her part, but it does illustrate how well-meaning reactions can land on the person who is disabled. "I didn't want to have to make other people feel better, which often happens," she explains.

Before Anne got Cheryl and when she was feeling depressed, Anne imagined her life would stretch into "a big grey emptiness." She could no longer read any of the thousands of books in her library, couldn't imagine having another romantic relationship, and thought she'd never travel again. "I just thought it was going to be a pretty lonely, solitary life." But when Cheryl arrived, Anne found she and the dog could travel together, and they took a trip to Costa Rica. She rebuilt her social life. "The dog smoothed everything over," she explains. "People weren't hesitant, as if somebody was having a great big house party (and they know how to do this here . . . you get seventy people in your house) they might not invite somebody who uses a wheelchair or a white cane for fear they would get hurt. But Cheryl and I would be there, so this business about the dog being your bridge out of segregation is a real thing."

When Anne was in her forties, in a bid to save her marriage, she had started running with her husband. It didn't work, but it did instill a long-standing fondness for being in motion. These days, her eyesight isn't good enough to run, it's too risky, but she is often seen energetically walking the trails and boardwalks around St. John's in the company of her dog. The winter throws a spanner in the works, however. "One of the reasons why I'm very resentful about the snow clearing situation in St. John's is because it's not just about getting from place to place and it's not just about physical activity. I think for a lot of people, getting outdoors and being able to move freely around their environment is a social determinant of health."

Anne is committed to staying active and it irks her that this defies some people's expectations about persons with disabilities. "People often think I'm a dog trainer because people have an expectation of what blind people move like—the slow shuffle, the looking down, you know? For some people, that is true; a person might be elderly, a person may have a disability besides blindness, all kinds of things. They could just be old. They could be depressed. They could have shoes that hurt. But they're not doing that simply because they can't see."

Anne and Cheryl spent more than a decade together. "She was my first guide dog, and if you talk to other people who have guide dogs, I think you'll find out that even if they've had six or seven dogs and loved them all, they always obsess on the first one." Cheryl's arrival marked a seismic shift in Anne's life. Now she has her second guide dog, a young Chocolate Lab named Purdy. "Cheryl's entry into my life was huge. It was like, 'Oh, thank God!' Purdy's was less dramatic," she says, "but Purdy continues the legacy."

Anne is a direct person, with an innate sense of justice, and she has become an outspoken disability activist. In April 2013, when a local cab driver refused to allow her in his cab because she had her dog with her, she filed a human rights complaint against the company and won. She gave a TED Talk that year entitled "License to Beg: Challenging Views of 'Legal' Blindness." She's run for office municipally and has been invited to run provincially. "My experience has been that governments say all the right things, but they don't honestly do anything," she says, adding, "I am very grassroots, so I don't mind afflicting the comfortable at all." Anne is not afraid to speak truth to power. "People who live with significant sight loss in Canada have a 70 percent unemployment rate, so it's a pretty daunting financial world to a person living with sight loss," she says. "The status quo is not working for most of us. I don't care who you are; if what I'm saying is true, I'm not going to be inhibited by anything."

Anne's renewed self-confidence and her activism stem from one place. "All of that came out of having a disability and getting that dog," she says. "I never imagined myself becoming a disability advocate. None of it would have happened without the dog."

Chance

Shell-Shocked

Julie's quiet, almost stoic, demeanour stood her in good stead as an RCMP constable. Born and raised in Calgary, Alberta, she is fifty-four years old, and has dealt with all manner of tragedies in her twenty-plus years with the Royal Canadian Mounted Police. But nothing could have prepared her for the events of March 3, 2005.

Julie was among the first officers to arrive on scene in the wake of the gruesome murder of four of her fellow officers. On one of the worst days in RCMP history, Constables Leo Johnston, Anthony Gordon, Brock Myrol and Peter Schiemann were shot by James Roszko on his farm near Mayerthorpe, Alberta. Roszko then shot and killed himself.

Mayerthorpe is a small community northwest of Edmonton, and the officers, known as the Fallen Four, were all friends of Julie's. Three were members of her tiny local Mayerthorpe

RCMP detachment of eight officers. Anthony Gordon was from Whitecourt detachment, just up the highway.

The day before the shootings, Julie had already been at Roszko's farm. Bailiffs had gone to the farm to repossess a truck, but Roszko had caught wind of it and taken off. Julie helped get the bailiffs onto the farm and rounded up two aggressive Rottweilers Roszco had set loose. She and her fellow officers then lay in wait for him to return. Julie had to leave at 3 a.m. to get some sleep before attending a court hearing that morning, and Peter Schiemann, who would replace her on the stakeout, had loaned her his tie for the court appearance because she had left hers in her car, which was still at the farm.

Later that morning, after court, she remembers hearing over the police radio that shots had been fired and that the four constables at the scene were missing. She and fellow officers rushed back to the farm to wait for the Emergency Response Team to arrive. Unbeknownst to them, all four officers already lay dead inside a Quonset hut on the farm.

Julie remembers very little of what she experienced that day. "I blocked quite a bit," she says, not an uncommon coping response to trauma. In the aftermath, she felt as though she was largely unsupported by the RCMP. Their response, she says, was, "Suck it up, Princess." In the aftermath she was isolated and shell-shocked. She soldiered on, but not without emotional repercussions.

Working as a constable had exposed Julie to some very tough situations. "I got called out to a bad crash," she remembers, "where a young girl passed away and a guy burnt to death. The father of the young girl was on scene, and it was very traumatic. You deal with that, and suicides, and everything just kind of builds on you, right? You start getting the nightmares and certain smells trigger you and certain noises trigger you—and *then* Mayerthorpe and everything went for shit."

Julie's dance with the shock waves of trauma began much earlier, during her first assignment as an Alexis First Nations Reserve police officer, an hour northwest of Edmonton. She was living just two minutes away from the reserve when she was brought in to assist in a fire she thought was in another RCMP detachment area. "I was going to back them up, and I came up the hill and I saw it was my house," Julie remembers. Inadvertently she broadcast her first reaction to every cop listening. "All you heard on the radio was, 'Fuck, it's my house!'" she recalls. Her house was totalled, and there were feline casualties. "It was quite the panic trying to get my animals out, but they were, of course, already . . ." she says, her voice trailing off. She lost two cats in the fire. Although no charges were laid, she believes it was arson and that she knows who set the fire. "This one gentleman, who was really not a nice person, came to my door one day asking to go out on a date, and I said to get the fuck off my property. And exactly a week later to the day, to the hour, my house burnt down."

Despite the impact of that tragedy, and others she had to cope with as part of her job, Julie didn't get a service dog until 2014—nine years after Mayerthorpe. Her best friend, a dog trainer, suggested it. "I was fucked up," Julie says, laughing dolefully. She was experiencing all of the classic PTSD symptoms: flashbacks, nightmares, depression, anxiety and not sleeping. She was beginning to hide from the world. "I wouldn't go anywhere unless I absolutely had to," she says. "My friend noticed that I'd turtle at home. She'd try and get me to come out, and I'd make excuses." When Julie did go out for something essential, like groceries, she'd often have a panic attack right in the middle of the store and have to flee.

Her first service dog was Saint, an Australian Shepherd she got as a puppy. He was good at understanding her emotional needs, but when he became overprotective and wouldn't let anyone near her, she had to retire him. She knew she still needed help. Her next dog was Chance, a Chocolate Lab who was trained by George Leonard at MSAR. Julie remembers making the trip to Winnipeg to meet George and his crew for the very first time. "I went to George's and he said, 'Okay, just go into the house. Go sit on the chair. Don't say a word,' and I did, and this Yellow Lab came up to me and was sniffing me, and he walked away. And then Chance came up and jumped into my lap. George said, 'Okay, put a leash on that dog. She's yours.'" George had about ten dogs in the house that day, and Julie could have gone home with a poodle, an Australian Shepherd or a Lab. But it was Chance, a Chocolate Lab with a chestnut-coloured coat and amber eyes, who chose Julie. "She just jumped up and said, 'I'm going to take care of you,' and she has ever since."

When asked if her dog saved her life, Julie declares, without hesitation, "Absolutely!" Julie found herself in a potentially dangerous headspace and, despite the therapy she was doing, she couldn't seem to get a handle on it. "Before I got Chance, I would get visions of myself holding a gun to my head. My psychologist was saying, 'Well, that's just stress, blah, blah blah,' but, you know, it's scary. I'm thinking, 'Am I actually going to pull that trigger one day?' When I got Chance, if I got these visions, she would bonk me and lick my hand and get me out of stuff like that. She wakes me up from my night terrors, and if I'm in a crowded room, she will literally pull me out of the room if I start to amp up. So in that way, she's pretty much saved my life, saying, 'Okay, Mumma, you take care of me, and I'll take care of you.' And here we are."

When she is in crowds and anxiety begins kicking in, Julie might not recognize it immediately, but Chance does, and it's her job to keep her owner safe. "I'll start sweating and start getting anxious, and I have a tic I'll start to do with my fingers, and she'll know it's time to go," Julie says, explaining that Chance is trained to recognize these signals and she's learned to pay attention to her dog. "I've got a leash that I have around my waist, and it goes to her. If she feels my heart rate or my blood pressure going up, she'll find the exit and get me out of there. I could be just zoned, and she'll be, 'Okay, Mumma, time to go,' and she'll pull me out of the room," Julie says. "She can feel everything down the leash. If I've got one hell of a grip on the leash, she'll just put the brakes on, and I'll keep walking and then I hit the end of the leash, not her," she says, laughing. "I go, 'What?' and then I've got to tell her that I'm okay." Chance helps ground Julie when her anxiety gets the best of her, and she also knows how to respond when nighttime becomes overwhelming. Chance sleeps in Julie's bed, and when she's getting unsettled and heading to a nightmare, Chance will sense it coming. "If she feels that I start moving around, she'll actually bonk on me and paw me and wake me up. And she'll start licking my face. There's a happy face right there saying, 'Everything's going to be okay.' It's quite remarkable."

Among their many skills, psychiatric therapy dogs are trained to ground their handler in unsettling situations, guide them away from a stressful event, "wake" them when they zone out, and interrupt them when they engage in repetitive behaviours, like Julie's tics.

Even though her dog has helped her manage her PTSD, she says she didn't get the right kind of support from her employer. "I fought with the RCMP since I got Chance, well, even before that when I had Saint. They would call Chance a pet even though she was a trained service dog. . . . I even went to Ottawa to see the commissioner of the RCMP to say this is bullshit."

Julie's relationship with the RCMP came to an inglorious end almost two years ago. "Yeah, I pretty much got booted because of it," she remembers bitterly. "I have trouble making phone calls and talking to people on the phone, so they put me in a unit where that's all I did because they didn't want anybody to see me with Chance." Julie says there were many other things she could have done that would not have required her to be on public view with a service dog. "I'm a twenty-year member; I can do a lot of stuff where I'm not on the road, like I could do search warrants, I could do this, that and the other thing," she says. "So it was a forced retirement."

Julie has made peace with her situation, although she's not happy with how things played out, and in her view, it was neither necessary nor elegant. "It's a kick in the pants, like, 'Get out the door. We don't want you anymore.'"

Since she left active duty, Julie keeps herself busy on her four-acre rural property. Her father, who's in his eighties, moved in with her not long ago. She loves her property, with its view of the mountains, and she lives in a virtual menagerie with a horse, a minimule, an alpaca, three cats and four dogs.

Chance is nine years old, and their ongoing partnership has more than a crisis management side to it. She and Julie are constant companions, best buddies. "I find that I'm better and better, just having her," Julie says.

In the not-too-distant future, she will have to find a replacement for her sidekick, who is getting close to service dog retirement age. While Chance will no longer be on active duty, she'll always have a place in Julie's home. Finding her successor will be an undertaking of life-or-death importance. If not for Chance, Julie believes, "I don't think I'd be here."

Montana

Super Quad

Long before a dog saved his life (more than once), Brad was a brash hotshot who loved nothing more than driving deep into the bush and hiking the backcountry of British Columbia. He was a twenty-seven-year-old ladies' man, TV producer and daredevil cameraman—the kind of guy who hung out of helicopters to get his shot. "I was a wild and crazy guy. I was the most eligible bachelor in Vancouver, according to *Vancouver Magazine*, one year. Yeah, I was a shit-hot cameraman, *just ask me*."

And then, on September 26, 1980, he had a catastrophic accident.

He and his best buddy, Norm, were driving on the Whistler highway, a couple of hours north of Vancouver. Back then the road up to Whistler was a rough one, more like a wagon trail, Brad remembers. He had taken his brand-new four-wheel-drive truck out for a run when he hit some gravel on the road and the truck spun out, rolling three and a half times and landing upside down on its roof, in a gully 150 feet off the road.

When they came to, Brad remembers, "the dust started to settle." He continues, "We were both upside down, but Norm was kind of in my lap, not looking at me, looking straight down and bleeding like crazy. He had cut his wrist—the sunroof had come in—and there was blood everywhere. And I'm looking at him and I said, 'Fuck, man, you're bleeding bad,' and he said, 'I know,' and put his hand on his wrist. And then he said, 'Are you okay?' and I said, 'Yeah, I think so.'" Norm crawled out of the truck, but when he got a good look, he realized that Brad was anything *but* okay. "It was at that moment that I realized I was actually looking out the back window of the truck and I was strapped in, facing forward. So, my head had come right around."

Brad's windpipe had been crushed. When the truck hit the ground, he says, "the seat belt snapped tight, held me up, the roof came in, I had no defence, it just crushed. So the seat belt broke my neck. Norm, because he wasn't wearing a seat belt, slid into my lap. I'm upside down, I'm wearing a seat belt. It created traction on my spine, so it let my head turn without breaking everything. The seat belt saved my life."

Brad's injuries were grave. Vertebrae C6 and C7 in his cervical spine had been pulverized and, if he even survived, he would be a quadriplegic. "Norm looked at me. I said, 'I can't breathe. I can't breathe.' And he reached up and took my chin—the doctors actually asked him later if he had medical training—but he reached up and he took my chin and he just turned my head and I felt my windpipe pop and suddenly I could breathe. And he said, 'Now you just need to stay like that. I've got to go find some help.'"

Brad passed out. When he woke, he was surrounded by six or seven firefighters trying to get him out of his truck. "One guy got in with me. I'm upside down and he crawls in and he's putting stuff around my neck and trying to stabilize me as best he can. And he said, 'We don't have the equipment to get you out of this car. We have to put it back on its wheels. I'm coming in there with you. I'm going to hold you as tight as I can.'" It was a risky move, but the only option if he was going to save Brad's life. The firefighter told him, "I can wiggle in, but I can't just drag you out. Your neck's broken. Your head's going to flop around. You're going to die. I can't have that. So we have to get the car up on the side, at least, and it'd be better if we flipped it right over.'" The firefighter wrapped himself around Brad in a bear hug, and the manoeuvre worked. They got the truck right side up, but the pain was so intense Brad passed out in shock.

In a best-case scenario, Brad would have been airlifted to a Vancouver hospital, but the local helicopter had been loaned to the fire service, so it was unavailable. The only option was to load him into an ambulance for a precarious journey down the mountain to a hospital in North Vancouver. Along the way, he flatlined twice. The first time, when the attendant assumed he was dead, Brad says, "Norm went ballistic and grabbed the attendant by the lapels, slammed him up against the side of the back doors, and said, 'What are you talking about? You're not shutting anything down!'" At that moment Brad woke, saw them fighting and asked them what the hell they were doing. It was a close call.

A team was waiting for them as they arrived at the hospital. "There happened to be a big meeting at that hospital discussing traumatic injury to the neck, and the best doctor in the whole frickin' world was there, Dr. Brian Hunt," Brad says. In short order, he was in an operating room, undergoing seven hours of surgery to stabilize his neck.

It was the beginning of a painful trek toward a new life. Brad was, in his words, "a super quad," meaning he had some movement in one of his hands. He endured brutal rehab and had to learn how to do everything again. "Learning how to get dressed. Learning how to eat. Learning how to be cool. Learning how to go on a date. Learning how to steal a kiss. It's hard to steal a kiss in a wheelchair." These were compelling reasons for a fellow who fancied himself a "man about town."

Given Brad's innate sense of bravado, being confined to a wheelchair cramped his style on every level, but he is a maverick of a man, and a stubborn one. As he says, "If anybody in the world was going to make it, if anybody was ever going to get out of this alive, it was me." And he had no intention of living an institutionalized life. While he was in a rehab hospital, he got himself kitted out with an accessible apartment, and much to the consternation of his health-care providers, he bought a black truck rigged up to be fully wheelchair accessible, with lifts and everything he would need to allow him to head to the back country again. "It was designed to go camping. They said, 'You don't really think you're going camping again, do you?' I said, 'Not only am I going camping, I'm going to be camping every chance I get.'"

Brad was trying to rebuild his personal and professional life so it had some semblance of the normal that predated his accident, but he was in a kind of denial. "I avoided disability. I didn't want to talk about it. I didn't want to see anybody with it. I didn't want to look in the mirror. All my mirrors were waist up. I didn't want to think about it." He went back to work, now as a producer and writer.

Nine years after his accident, Brad went on his first date with the woman who would become his wife. Theirs was a storybook love affair. He first met Tarren, an actress, at a crowded industry party. He thought she was the most gorgeous brunette he'd ever seen, but she was taken. Months later, always one for big gestures and determined to win her over, he orchestrated a fictitious casting call. The minute she saw him she knew what he was up to, but now single, she agreed to go out with him.

Already smitten, Brad fell even harder for her because Tarren chose to be with him despite his disability. "She knew what a daunting task this was going to be, and she did it anyway." From their first date they were inseparable, and four months after he'd first laid eyes on her they were living together. It is an enduring relationship that has lasted ever since.

Brad's professional life was also about to undergo a big change. In a chance encounter in an elevator, he ran into Rick Hansen, a Canadian disability advocate who had become paraplegic when he was thrown from the back of a pickup truck. Rick was organizing Independence '92, a massive international congress on disability, and he asked Brad to be project manager. Brad jumped at the chance. He loved working on a grand scale, and this type of producing work was right up his alley.

Brad had extensive experience as a producer, but he was a newbie to the disability movement, despite his own personal experience in the years since his accident. He was blown away by what he experienced. The meeting, at Canada Place in Vancouver, was massive, with 2,700 delegates from around the world, almost all of whom had disabilities. "Some were so seriously disabled I could not believe my eyes," Brad remembers. At the end of the first plenary session, he waited outside the meeting hall, hoping to see happy delegates emerge. "Finally, the door opens and nothing happens. And I wait a minute and then I swear to God, if Gandalf exists, this guy comes out, long beard and old clothes, and he's got a wooden staff and he plants it on the ground and he pulls his legs forward on the ground, and he plants it on the ground and everyone behind him is totally respectful, giving him all the space he needs.

"So I rolled up to Gandalf and I said, 'You know, we put together a whole brace shop where you can get braces and canes and crutches and everything you need brand-new, no cost. It's all sponsored. You gotta go down and get set up man, it'd be way better for you.'

"The next day at the end of the conference, here comes Gandalf, planting and pulling. I rolled up. 'So, what happened? Why aren't you in braces? Why don't you have proper canes and crutches?' He said, 'I went down, they were so great. Look what they did.' And he turned over his staff and they had put a rubber cap on the bottom. He said, 'I couldn't get any grip on these floors.' And he said, 'That's just changed my life.' And I thought to myself, 'We just spent five bucks and changed his life. Because we—who the hell *are we* to *tell him* what he needs?' It changed the way I think."

He shares one more story about shifting his perspective on disabilities and what people need, about a delegate named Yuri, who had no legs. "He arrived on a skateboard and he had leather gloves to push himself around. He was the media darling. He had enough English and he knew he had a role to play. They were going to buy him a wheelchair, and they had these big events and fundraising events. A wheelchair for him was going to cost around four grand. And this big campaign happened, and they bought a really nice, cherry-coloured, beautiful wheelchair. And he did the media and thanked them profusely, and said,

'Without your help, I don't know what I'd do.' And then the media went away and the cameras went off, and he turned to me and said, 'I can't use this thing. I live in Russia. There are no curb ramps, there's no accessible doorways. If you want to help me, give me a case of leather gloves.' I just went, 'Holy shit. Are you serious?' And he said, 'Yeah.' I traded him a case of leather gloves for the wheelchair, and I gave the wheelchair to someone who actually needed it."

The conference was an epiphany for Brad. "My head is just swimming because I'd spent the last ten years avoiding all these conversations, not having anything to do with it. Suddenly, with Independence '92, I was seeing a whole other world that I had quite successfully pretended I wasn't part of." When Justin Dart, considered the godfather of the Americans with Disabilities Act, took Brad aside and encouraged him to shift his work life focus over to accessibility, Brad took the advice to heart. Before too long, that was a full-time gig, and Brad became an international access consultant who specialized in large public buildings and public events, including the 2010 Olympics. It was heady stuff.

But over time, the travel was really tough on his body. Because he had the use of one of his hands, he was able to get around in a manual wheelchair. But making his way around airports and large event sites was draining. "Even if I am a super quad," Brad says, "I'm going to run out of gas."

He had to admit he needed help. Brad was adamant that he didn't want a human attendant, but what about a dog? He could see himself relying on some canine help. And when he saw a TV ad for service dogs, he applied. Eighteen months later, the phone rang and they had a dog for him.

Brad's first dog was a very big, very strong Golden Retriever. "Montana was a pulling machine and a retrieving machine. I needed a big dog that I could grab on to and say, 'Pull,' and we'd go a hundred miles an hour through the airport. That's a very special skill." Having a dog would also spare his wife, Tarren, some of the typical attendant care duties. For instance, Montana could help him with personal needs, and that was important to Brad. "Here's where the dog changed my life. By being dependent on him, *I* became independent in life."

Becoming quadriplegic hadn't dampened Brad's love of the outdoors, and more incredibly, he still went camping, solo! It was his form of empowerment, but it could be downright dangerous for a man in a wheelchair, no matter how intrepid. "I love road trips; my favourite thing in the world is to drive off into the desert. But that meant going into a place with no cell coverage, no phone, no nothing, by myself. That would drive Tarren crazy, just crazy, but she said, 'I can't stop you.' Now, suddenly, I wasn't alone anymore, I had Montana. Little things wouldn't fuck me up. Dropping the keys under a truck wouldn't end my life, end my day. You know, bad things could happen and I wasn't alone. Montana was there, and he was so capable."

The freedoms afforded him by Montana also brought useful responsibilities. Dogs can't feed themselves or take themselves out for a pee, so Brad still had to get up and tend to his dog's needs, even on his low days. "When Montana comes in and sits at the base of the bed and just gives you the eyes, you're getting up. And even if you're really hurting that day, if your shoulders are shot or you've got a wicked bladder infection, it doesn't matter because your best friend now needs help. And suddenly that tightens the bond, but it creates a sense of purpose for you."

Beyond the profound difference dogs made in his life on a daily basis, there have also been several times where Brad's dogs have saved him from serious harm, if not worse. One night, having worked very late, he and Montana were heading back to his van, which he had absent-mindedly parked at the end of an unsafe alley in Vancouver's Downtown Eastside. It hadn't occurred to him that he could be heading right into danger. He remembers Montana becoming uncharacteristically agitated, and looking back on it, he says he really wasn't paying enough attention. "I happened to look up just in time to see a large, presumably homeless, man who jumped out from behind a dumpster in a very, very aggressive manner. He had bad intent, there is no question in my mind. I felt that he was going to try to tip me out of the chair." Service dogs are trained not to show any aggression. But when the man from the shadows made like he was going for Brad, Montana did what he was trained *not* to do. "He planted himself in that ancient wolf stance and he bared his teeth and he went, 'Whoof!!' And the guy went, 'Holy shit,' and stepped back. 'Good evening, sir,' he said. 'I just want to know if you need any help.' And Montana held that post. He stayed in that low crouch, that wolf's stance, ready to pounce, ready to spring, not baring teeth, but with a little grrr. And I said, 'No, thank you very much. I don't need any help,' and he turned and walked away." Service dogs are never supposed to show aggression toward anyone, but that night Montana demonstrated tremendous emotional intelligence when he betrayed his own training, protecting his owner from the possibility of harrowing consequences. "Montana saw danger and he was not going to tolerate that for a second. And he never did it again. Now, mind you, I never did anything that stupid again!"

Some years later, Brad was on another solo outing when he got himself into trouble. "I live in a rural area and I'm out in my chair and I go through a little bog I shouldn't have, and I sink right to my hubs. This chair wasn't moving an inch and I'm about a kilometre away from the house. This predated cell phones. I'm stuck, I'm not going an inch." He enlisted Montana's help, saying, "Listen to me. This is important. It's important. I need you to go find Tarren. Go find Tarren. Go find Tarren now!!" Montana took off. He made his way back home, and the instant he walked in without Brad, Tarren knew something was really wrong. She told him to go find Brad and followed as he led her back to where Brad was stranded. Without Montana's help, Brad says, his situation could very quickly have become dire.

Montana lived for thirteen years and was in service to Brad for ten. Losing him was heartbreaking, Brad says. Since then, dogs have remained an integral part of his life and he's had two more dogs. Remembering how this conversation began, he says, "In answer to, 'Did my dog save my life?' Yes! Every goddamn day! Every single day."

Connie

Braving Bullies

Laura, who has always been visually impaired, had lost most of her sight by the time she was in her early twenties. When she was twenty-three years old, she got her first guide dog. That was more than forty years ago; since then, she has had nine guide dogs. Each one—Champ, Angel, Ginger, Jetta, Sunni, Hanna, Anouk, Farley and Connie—has kept her safe from harm. But it is her current dog, Connie, who literally saved her life.

Laura was born in 1958, when there was little support for children with special needs and their families. Accessibility was hardly even on the agenda, let alone discussed. Canada passed the Blind Persons Act in 1951, but it was very new and there was still a tendency to segregate the blind community. "I came from a time when it was shaming to have a disabled child," she says. Laura had no connections in the blind community, and she felt isolated and unsure of herself. Disability activism was in its infancy and there were few examples available to help children figure out who they wanted to be. In Laura's case, it meant she tried to stay under the radar. "I was very timid and very shy and didn't want to rock the boat," she says.

Laura remembers school being difficult. She was accepted to W. Ross Macdonald School in Brantford, Ontario, a school for blind children that went from kindergarten right through high school, but her parents opted not to send her. She was put into the mainstream Catholic school system, and it didn't go well, partly because educators tended to segregate disabled children. "I was really struggling in school because I couldn't see," she says. "There wasn't any awareness back then of kids with special needs—they cloistered them into a different group." Given the impediments she faced, it's not surprising that Laura dropped out of high school before she could graduate. Impressively, she did have the grit to eventually go back to school, getting her GED and going on to complete some college-level work.

The lack of infrastructural support in the 1970s made it tough for a young woman with unique needs to manage in a sighted world. Until she had a guide dog, Laura was getting around by using a white cane. "I know a number of people who are magnificent with their cane. I'm not," she says. Even the simplest tasks, like crossing the street, grocery shopping, or getting on a bus, were stressful and sometimes downright perilous.

Her life changed markedly for the better when she got her first guide dog in the early 1980s. Venturing out with Champ by her side gave her new-found independence and the ability to move more freely in the world. Laura, like many young people starting out, was working at jobs that didn't pay very well. She economized by renting lodgings that were a little rough around the edges. Having a dog meant that she felt more secure about being in parts of town she might otherwise have avoided. "I'm not sure I would have wanted to live on my own all those years in apartment buildings that were kind of sketchy, just to save money," she says.

Despite her new-found freedom, her life was still studded with challenges. There were times when the simple act of using public transit put her into frightening situations. "I used to get off the bus in downtown Oshawa and I had to walk past skinheads because they always congregated by the bus stops in this area. I remember being pushed off the sidewalk and onto the road and complaining to the bus driver. He said, 'There's nothing I can do about it,'" she says. "It was really terrifying for me. But because I had a dog, I felt safer, because she would ensure my safety."

While her guide dogs made daunting situations more manageable, they sometimes made Laura a target. She often had to cope with unprovoked and unexpectedly senseless situations. "I've lived in areas where young kids thought it was funny to ride their bikes up to me when I was walking with my dog and slam on the brakes in front [of us] to see what the dog would do. Or throw rocks at the dog. That's happened to me a number of times," she says.

Her dogs have helped her manage other problematic situations. "I had a couple of dogs that were so in tune with my emotions, they knew when I was upset, and they'd try to comfort me. When I was working in a call centre—that's a toxic technical sweatshop—my dog seemed to know when I wasn't having a good day, and he would get off his bed and he would come over and put his head on my lap."

The other reality Laura has had to deal with numerous times is the grief that comes with giving a dog up. When guide dogs reach a certain age, they have to be retired, and it's not easy to let go. "You develop a very strong bond with them," she says.

She remembers meeting people who told her that the grief they felt losing their guide dog was comparable to losing a child. "It's very difficult to explain to people the connection that you have," she says.

As Laura was becoming braver with each dog by her side, she was also discovering her inner advocate. Since 1976, blind people have had the right—by law—to have a guide dog, without being barred from public spaces or housing. When cab drivers and shopkeepers didn't know or didn't care to understand this, Laura would set them straight by quoting the Blind Persons' Rights Act. If that didn't work, she would resort to tougher tactics. "I was pretty much kicked out of almost every store I tried to enter," she recalls. "I called the police a lot and it got to the point where the police said, 'Just tell them to call us!'" To be her own advocate didn't come easily. "I don't want a confrontation in a store or something like that, so I try to educate. But then there's the other me that says, 'I am so tired of this. I just want it to stop.' And it just feels like you could spend your life outside the Human Rights Commission saying, 'This is wrong!'"

Laura has found the courage to speak up in other situations as well. Once, when the car broke down, she and her husband called a tow truck. The driver refused to let her dog into the cab of the truck with them. "He said, 'No! Dogs have to go in the back,' and I said, 'No, she's not,'" Laura remembers. She prevailed. Laura called the towing company to complain, and when the driver was instructed to let the dog ride with them, he had to comply. "He was just so mad that my dog guide had to be in his truck." In another instance, she encountered what could be called "sighted privilege" while waiting to make a purchase in a clothing store. "At the counter somebody came along and poked me in the arm and said, 'The baby.' And I said, 'Pardon?' She said, 'The baby's afraid of dogs. You have to go.' I said, 'That's unfortunate. I'm not going anywhere,'" Laura remembers. Her husband jokes that not only has she come out of her shell, but she's tenacious about defending the things she believes in. It's taken decades and lots of practice. "I don't think I really found my voice till I turned sixty," she says.

Laura got her current dog, Connie, in the spring of 2022, but they got off to a shaky start. During the COVID pandemic, Connie had been with a foster owner for two years, after which she'd spent a year in a kennel. She was already three years old by the time she arrived in Laura's life. "The first week I had her, I wasn't sure I was going to keep her because she wasn't working for me," Laura says. "She'd been tossed around a few times, and I think she thought, 'Is this just another stopover and I'm going to go somewhere else?'" It didn't take long for Laura to see that Connie was a very clever dog, and with a little help from the school that had originally trained her, they got themselves onto solid ground. "She can outsmart me, she's so smart. I knew I had to work hard, and she had to work hard. And that's the true relationship of a dog guide handler and their dog."

Six months later, Laura and Connie had a potentially disastrous brush with danger. Just before Christmas, Laura was out walking with a blind friend and they both had their dogs with them. They came to a busy multi-lane intersection on an especially hectic and noisy day. There was a lot of traffic, but it was a crossing Laura had made many times before. Laura was in the lead and instructed Connie to step off the curb and into the crossing. They got about halfway through the intersection when the dog came to an abrupt halt. Seconds later a car whizzed past them, so close Laura felt the air move and the heat of the car's engine as it sped by. Shaken, Laura regrouped and finished crossing the street when the friend she was walking with heard a woman shouting to them to stop. "I was still reverberating from it," Laura remembers. The woman, who had witnessed everything, told Laura, "If you hadn't stopped, you would have been killed. I have never seen anybody scream through there so fast." Laura began shaking, and crying, but when she hugged the dog to thank her, Connie was unfazed. "It's like second nature to them," Laura says. "Kind of, 'Yeah, that's okay. Let's just keep going forward.'"

Remembering that incident reminded her of a winter morning when an inattentive driver didn't see Laura and another of her dogs behind his car and began backing out of his driveway. The dog, seeing the car heading for them, bolted forward, pulling her out of the way. "You know, that's just an average day for a guide dog," Laura says. "There's probably a lot of things that all my dogs have done that I don't have awareness of, just that I got from point A to point B."

Laura laughs and adds, "There's a saying among my friends and me: 'Any time you come back from a walk still alive is a good walk!'"

Buddy

Grief's Goodness

Joan met her late husband in the summer of 2002, while at an Indigenous Ceremony in South Dakota. Joan is a member of Woptura Tiospaye of the Oglala Sioux Nation and had been Sun Dancing, a gruelling spiritual practice that goes on for four days. When she finished her own Sun Dance and returned to her campsite, her voluminous long hair was full of branches and twigs from lying in the grass when she had taken breaks during the Ceremony. When her friends asked if she needed anything to eat or drink, sustenance was not the first thing on her mind. She said, "I just want a brush. I want to get all this stuff out of my hair." Before she knew it, Harold Johnson, whom she didn't know but who was staying at the next campsite, had found a brush and was standing behind her, brushing her hair. "You're in a kind of hypersensitive state at that point," she says, "and it felt so gentle and kind and respectful."

It was the beginning of an intense long-distance courtship. At the time they met, Joan was working for the Ontario Federation of Indian Friendship Centres as their justice coordinator, and Harold was working as legal counsel for a labour union. He was a handsome man who wore his long white hair in braids; Joan was petite with a beautiful smile. They had tons in common and talked to each other constantly on the phone. Three months after they met, they were married. Joan was fifty and Harold was forty-four, and while they had both been married before, Joan never doubted it was the right thing to do. "I thought, okay, this is my last go at this. If I don't get it right this time, then I'm done," she says. "As it turns out I got it right, I found my soulmate."

Eventually they moved three hundred kilometres north of Saskatoon and lived in a tent on his family's trapline for about six months while they cleared the land. Harold built them a cabin, where they lived for almost two decades—each of them becoming reconnected with the land.

Harold's mother was Cree, his father Swedish. As he said in a CBC Radio interview, "I was this half-breed from northern Saskatchewan—nothing was expected from me except that I fail." He was tenacious, never taking no for an answer, and before becoming a writer and lawyer, he was many things—a trapper, logger and miner, before going to Harvard to do graduate work in law. While he was a Crown prosecutor, he wrote the book *Firewater: How Alcohol Is Killing My People (and Yours)*. He became disillusioned with how the judiciary dealt with Indigenous people and quit law to take up writing full time, producing important books on justice.

He was also a planner. When he was diagnosed with stage 4 lung cancer, he did everything he could to fight for his health but had to concede that he might not survive this prodigious foe. And so, he began to plan for a future when he was no longer around—Joan's future.

That is how Buddy, a long-haired Jack Russell Terrier, came into their lives. Ostensibly the dog was to be Harold's companion, but Joan says that Harold, ever the strategist, had longer-range plans. Harold found a breeder through a veterinarian friend and "he made a special order for Buddy," Joan remembers. "Harold didn't know how much time he had at that point, but he knew he had limited time. I really think that he was planning to have a buddy for me, as well as for him." Buddy weighs about fifteen pounds and has a kind of rumpled look—with wiry caramel and white hair, brown splotches of colour on his pink skin, and a black button nose and eyes. In no time Harold and Joan were besotted with him. "I've had lots of dogs in my life, lots of dogs! Buddy is different," she exclaims. "I mean, he's sentient. And I really mean that. He is so smart!"

Part two of Harold's plan was to move them away from their remote cabin to a place where Joan would not be isolated in the wake of his death. That led them to a little house on one of BC's Gulf Islands. It seemed like a wild option to Joan. "I would never have picked Gabriola, ever. It was his choice. He put me here."

In 2020, they packed up house in Saskatchewan and drove their RV, with Buddy in tow, more than three thousand kilometres across the country to their new home. It was a huge move. "I had left all the people that I worked with, everybody that I was close to. My family wasn't here. I didn't have any friends here. And it was in the middle of COVID," Joan says. It may have been an inopportune time to begin a new life, but Joan says in retrospect that Harold knew what he was doing. He had planned the move so they would be living in a paradise that was rural but wasn't remote.

Harold died on February 9, 2022, at the age of sixty-eight. The hole he left behind was huge. Being alone in a relatively new place was tough on Joan. "My family wasn't here. My friends weren't here," she says. If not for Buddy, she might have returned to Ontario, where her family is. Over time, she adjusted to living by herself on Gabriola, and slowly began to realize it was just the right place for her to heal. "It's safe and it's quiet. I have people if I need them, but I don't have to be around people. It's a beautiful spot, surrounded by stuff that feeds my spirit like the ocean and trees and mountains."

This is where her relationship with Buddy became a lifeline. When Joan got outside for walks with Buddy, it kept her connected to the world and it gave her contemplative space and time, which she needed in the days and weeks following Harold's death. While the adverse impact of isolation and loneliness on a person's overall health is well documented, studies are beginning to find that in the wake of losing a loved one, the company of an animal can be more helpful that any other support. "On my walks with Buddy, that's when I process things the most," she says. "I needed to figure out, okay, what's in the next chapter of my life? And if Buddy hadn't been there . . ." Her voice trails off. "Buddy certainly has been a lifesaver to me. He really has." His companionship also insured that she wasn't paralyzed by sorrow, if only because she had to put on her duds and go outdoors several times a day, inclement weather or not. "Because of Buddy, I'm out every day, rain or shine, doesn't matter. Whereas, if it wasn't for Buddy, I probably would just say, 'Okay, it's raining today, I'm not going out,'" she says, laughing at how constraining that would be, given the wet weather on Gabriola.

The kind of love Joan found with Harold was a once-in-a-lifetime thing, and she's not looking to replace it with anyone. But somehow, Buddy has a way of reminding Joan every day about the beauty of unconditional love from another creature. Well, perhaps not entirely *un*conditional—Joan smiles as she says, "He *is* a little demanding, he does want me to play, he does want me to go for walks, he does want me to pay attention to him, and he does want to eat. But even more than that, I think what he wants is love. And all the love that I have to give him, he can take it and it doesn't make him spoiled. It's reciprocal."

Interacting with Buddy has led to some surprising insights into her own inner journey. She cites an instance when she was holding Buddy and he was making a kind of humming sound. She made the sound back to him, and he repeated it back to her. She sees this kind of exchange of vibrations between them as a way of learning new ways of communicating. "I think this is a really important point for me in terms of spiritual growth—to recognize that he's my friend. I don't treat him like a baby. I treat him like the being that he is. He helps me in my spiritual understanding that we're all connected and we're all interdependent." Joan alludes to the Lakota prayer, All My Relations, which ends with, "We are in the circle of life together, co-existing, codependent, co-creating our destiny. One, not more important than the other. One nation evolving from the other and yet dependent upon the one above and the one below. All of us part of the Great Mystery."

And, perhaps just as importantly at a time when it could be in short supply, Buddy delivers to her a simple sense of unalloyed joy. He sleeps on her bed and wakes her early every morning. She laughs, thinking about his excitement as he jumps around, seeming to ask her, "How can you not be excited or grateful that you're here for another day?" She adds, "Buddy's a free spirit. He's the most amazing being that I've ever experienced."

Tinsley

Gully Save

When Cameron (Cam) went through heartbreak at the end of a seven-year romance, he knew the salve for his broken heart would be a new puppy. When he picked her up on Valentine's Day, he told the breeder, "This dog's going to save my life." And she did, twice. The first time was an emotional rescue. The second time would be even more dramatic.

Cam grew up in Vermont, in a pastoral part of the state that hugs the border with New Hampshire. His parents bought a farm in 1990, and Cam was born not long after. When he was six, his parents began breeding Shiloh Shepherds, a rare American breed that looks like a larger, more wolfish version of a German Shepherd. "We had seven of them at one point, running through the fields and going into town, always in the back of a pickup," Cam remembers.

At twenty-one, in his final year of college, Cam's idyllic life blew apart when his fifty-five-year-old father, whom he adored, died of a massive heart attack while working in the fields. As a boy, Cam and his father were inseparable, Cam hanging out in the farm's fields, riding his dirt bike alongside his father's tractor. When Cam was old enough, he began to work with his dad doing custom field work for other farms around Vermont and New Hampshire. When Cam played football in high school and college, his father made it a priority to be at all his games, sometimes driving for almost an hour and a half to be there. "I don't know how he did it with all the farm work, but he did it because he was supportive. It was great."

His father was the glue that held the family together, and his death ripped the family apart. Cam says relations between himself, his older sister, and his mother became somewhat dysfunctional. He still lives in a house on the family's 120-acre property and, as he did with his father, works on other people's farms clearing the fields and doing trail work. Now thirty-two, he is tall and slender with dark hair and a big beard; a solitary person with a quiet demeanour. He struggles with depression and anxiety, and when he and his girlfriend split up, he felt isolated and unhappy and he knew that he wanted—needed—a canine friend. He chose to get another Shiloh Shepherd, and the moment he set eyes on Tinsley, a newborn puppy, it was love at first sight.

Tinsley's colouring is a peachy tan with a dusting of black, and he has gentle eyes and a black muzzle. To the untrained eye, Tinsley looks very much like a German Shepherd. Shilohs are a newer breed, a cross between a German Shepherd and Alaskan Malamute; they were bred to be companion animals, with a gentle temperament, which was exactly what Cam needed.

He and Tinsley are together from the minute they wake up in the morning until the day ends. She goes to work with him, and having sole responsibility for her keeps him on track, even when he's having an off day. "She helps me get going. We get outside and go for hikes and walks. She keeps me on my toes and more alive, in a sense. Whenever I spend time with her, I get grounded again."

One January night in 2022, what began as an agreeable evening out with a friend took a dark turn. And if not for Tinsley, it could have had a much nastier outcome. Cam and a friend, Justin, had gone out to a local Chinese restaurant for some dinner and a few drinks. They were discussing some business opportunities, and both had taken their dogs along with them.

It was a cold night, with a skiff of snow on the ground. Heading home at about 10 p.m., Cam lost control of his truck, crashing it into the guardrail on an off-ramp from the highway. The truck rolled six or seven times and landed upside down in a gulley in a wooded area. It was totalled. Both men were knocked unconscious, but the dogs, uninjured, got out of the truck and headed up toward the highway. Justin's American Bulldog went one way and was sadly hit on the highway and died. But Tinsley, who had gone the opposite way, made it up the highway and crossed out of Vermont into New Hampshire on a narrow bridge going over the Connecticut River, where she was spotted by locals who alerted police. When the state trooper who responded found Tinsley on the bridge and got close to her, she wouldn't let him within six or eight feet. Cam says he learned later that as the police car got close, she'd look back, and start running as if beckoning him to follow her. Tinsley led them right to the wreck, which was obscured from view. "She comes running over to the bank and right behind there's flashing lights and the cops are coming," Cam remembers. "That's how police got to us so soon, because we were down in a ditch and my truck was rolled right up against some trees."

"We were already hypothermic when they got to us, because we had been knocked out for a while," Cam says. "I woke up before Justin did, and he was sprawled . . ." Cam's voice trails off for a second before he continues, "I don't really like to relive this . . . everything was upside down and I had a lot of pressure on me. It's like I was caught in some way. I was trying to gather what was going on, and then I knew something wasn't right. And I wiggled out and dragged him out. At that point he was in pain. But he's a tough guy, he is one tough guy! I tell you what, I just can't believe that we both survived." One of the firefighters who were first on the scene said that while EMS treated the young men, Tinsley sat calmly nearby.

Justin was badly injured, with a fractured leg and vertebra, and Cam took it hard. Even now, considering what happened, he says, "I don't know what I would have done to myself if something more happened to him. I probably would be in the psych ward, or I don't know how I would deal . . ." His voice trails off again. "But I actually saw him two weeks after the accident and, being tough as he is, he was plowing snow."

Cam was charged with driving under the influence, and he lost his licence for a year. He and Justin remain good friends. And Tinsley and Cam remain as close as ever. "She's my guardian angel," he says, smiling.

Imari

Devoted Diva

The winter she was nine years old, Elizabeth had a freak accident while she and her friends were playing in the snow. One child threw a snowball that hit Elizabeth, causing her to lose her vision. Quite remarkably, she says, "It didn't bother me that I was losing my vision. I'm not even sure I understood it."

Elizabeth is from a big Newfoundland family. When she was ten, Elizabeth's parents sent her to the Halifax School for the Blind. Getting out of her parents' house was a reprieve from a dangerous situation where she had to deal with her father's sexual, mental and emotional tyranny. "I was from a very abusive home, so when I went away to school, I got away from that," Elizabeth says. "The abuse stopped because then other people would know, right? I was never bothered after that."

For the next seven years, Elizabeth was away at school most of the year, and she loved it there. "I went away and my life really opened up. It was amazing," she remembers. "Leaving home was a great adventure for me," she says. "As soon as I got there, I had friends, and I'd never really had friends before. We weren't allowed to bring people home, and we weren't allowed to go to someone else's house because then we'd find out that what was happening wasn't normal."

The aim of the school was to enable students to be self-sufficient, and Elizabeth learned to cook and bake, and even to read Braille, although it didn't come naturally to her. "They taught us how to do laundry. Every weekend a different room had to prepare a meal. We had to go do the shopping, plan a meal, and whatever we made had to be made from scratch . . . so they taught us all that. And they taught us how to be efficient." The orientation of the school set Elizabeth on a course toward being independent.

When she graduated at age seventeen, Laura returned to St. John's to her parents' home, but she was determined to get away as soon as she could. When she was nineteen, she heard about some local training for a medical Dictaphone typist and she jumped at it, never looking back. It was there that she met her first husband, who was also blind.

Elizabeth lived without a guide dog until she was in her forties. She didn't really like dogs and thought they were "stinky critters," but she grew increasingly frustrated about having to live by someone else's schedule and rely on others to get around. When a blind girlfriend introduced her to *her own* guide dog, Elizabeth realized that she, too, would benefit from having some canine help.

At the age of forty-five, Elizabeth got her first guide dog, a Lab named Imari. "She was a Yellow Lab, but she was pure white. She was beautiful, she shone, and everybody said she just glowed." Elizabeth jokes about Imari's vanity. "She thought she was a princess. She was so vain that if someone wanted to take her picture, she would pose. Her ear would go up, her nose would go up."

Almost overnight, what had been an extremely sedentary life for Elizabeth was transformed. Within weeks of being paired with Imari, Elizabeth had dropped twenty pounds. "When I got the dog, I was out for two hours every morning and two hours every night. Before that I went out maybe two hours a month. I was lazy." Elizabeth is five foot one, and since she became a dog owner, she has dropped from 265 pounds down to 152 pounds. "It made me way more independent, giving me way more confidence, and I didn't get lost," she says. Although taken with her new companion, it took Elizabeth a while to feel confident about this new relationship. "It was very scary being expected to follow an animal. It took me about two weeks to make the mental adjustment before I could actually trust her, because I'd never used a dog and I thought, 'What if she sees a cat?' Stuff like that," Elizabeth says.

Building the confidence to fully trust Imari paid off in what could have been a tragic situation. Elizabeth remembers it vividly. One day as she was walking alongside a four-lane road in Belleville, a smallish city in Ontario where she now lives, she got to a busy corner and she and Imari started into the intersection. By this point, she says, "I had lots of confidence with the dog, I totally trusted her, and I knew I had the light. We got maybe three-quarters of the way across, and some fool ran the light. I was probably close enough to touch the car. I could feel the wind. But I didn't panic. Imari stiffened, then turned to the right and took me back to the sidewalk," she says. "She saved me, actually." When Elizabeth and Imari were safely out of harm's way, a woman came running up to them saying, "I just saw what happened. You nearly got hit! You had the right of way." Elizabeth said to her, "I don't think that would have mattered if she had killed me."

Elizabeth says that once she had praised the dog for doing a good job and was confident that Imari was okay to continue working that day, they resumed their walk. "I've seen some dogs not even work when something like that happens—they can't because of the stress. But because I was calm, she was calm, and I gave her a cookie and told her she was a good girl and went on my way to Tim Hortons."

Elizabeth remembers another close call she had in the late fall, when she and Imari were out walking a trail in the early evening. She was heading home when she heard something, and to this day she doesn't know whether it was a person or an animal. Imari growled. She had never heard her dog growl, because service dogs are not supposed to growl or bark, so it was unsettling. Elizabeth hissed a warning into the air, saying, "Don't do anything stupid. She's trained to go for the crotch. I don't know who you are or what you want, but my dog feels very uncomfortable with you. Don't advance towards me because I will let her go and you will pay. So don't be stupid." Although Elizabeth didn't hear anyone, she could smell something, but she "couldn't tell if it was an animal or a person. When you can't see, you just don't know." Elizabeth maintained her calm, but Imari wasn't a happy dog. "She growled again and took a step, and I said, 'No!' and made her sit. The whole time the dog was growling in her throat, very uncomfortable. I still wasn't afraid yet because it hadn't come towards me, whatever it was. So I said out loud, 'I'm leaving now. If you attempt to follow me, I will let the dog go. Understand that! Stay where you are, and you'll be fine.' Then I said to Imari, 'Let's go,' and she took off at a run. I was actually running! So she was that scared. I don't know what it was or what she felt threatened by, but I feel like she saved my life that night too."

Elizabeth had Imari for about eight years, until the dog developed cancer and had to be retired as a working dog. Elizabeth's second support dog was a Black Lab named Mack, an eighty-pound gentle giant, and it was he who intervened when Elizabeth fell into a precarious diabetic crash. She was lying on her bed and her blood sugar levels had dropped, and she was conscious but couldn't get up, couldn't make her body move. Elizabeth says, "The dog went under my shoulders and sat me up, I swear to God, so that my feet were hanging off the bed. And I thought, 'Okay, thank you. Now what do I do?' and I fell back because I wasn't strong enough to sit up." Mack became agitated and started barking, which support dogs are trained not to do unless there's a crisis, and then raced down and got Elizabeth's husband Pete, who is also blind. Once Pete had discerned what was happening, he got her some fruit juice and she rallied. Elizabeth says that if she had been left alone she could have drifted into diabetic shock or died.

Elizabeth is matter-of-fact in her retelling of these stories, punctuating them by saying she isn't easy to frighten. But there is still a sense of well-placed awe in her voice when she describes how two well-trained service dogs, Imari and Mack, saved her from certain peril, ensuring that she dodged danger time after time.

Snoopy

Military Fallout

Shirley is a tiny person, standing just an inch over five feet. She's a bundle of positive energy, with an impish sense of humour and an infectious laugh that infiltrates many of her stories. Given the fallout from what she experienced during her time in the Canadian military, it is nothing short of a miracle that she laughs at all or that she has even survived. For that, she gives her dog Snoopy full credit. "Honestly, I would not be alive today if it wasn't for her."

Shirley was born in 1965 in a small town in central Nova Scotia. She is the daughter of Chinese immigrants who entered the country through the Pier 21 receiving station in Halifax. Her parents opened the first Chinese restaurant in their small town, and some of her favourite memories are of spending time there. "As a kid I used to hang out in the restaurant with my mom and dad in the mornings, and even as a teenager I used to hang out with them on weekends," she says. "I really am the luckiest person in the world. I had the most amazing parents. They weren't perfect, but they raised me with such strong values and ethics. The kindest people you'd ever meet." But things were complicated. Her mother spoke very little English and had serious mental health issues, and there were fissures within the family. Shirley stays in touch with two of her siblings—a sister who also went into the military and a brother who became a cop and did undercover police work—but she is completely estranged from the other two and doesn't offer an explanation for why.

Early on Shirley knew that she wanted to be in the military. As a kid she joined the cadets, then the reserve forces, and at age twenty-one she joined the regular forces, where she became a full-time employee. It was the beginning of a rich and varied professional life.

Her early years in the military were spent with units that did not put her in peril—her postings were with transport, and she got to see parts of western Canada that she didn't know as a Maritimer. She spent six months in Chilliwack, BC, where her gang of new recruits were having a good time, on and off the clock. "It's a good thing it was only six months, or I would have been an alcoholic. It was a good time. You know, your first posting, you're in the nice, warm climate and with all your buddies that you went through basic and your trades training with." Then she was moved to Edmonton, where she spent six years, and Camp Borden in Ontario, where she spent eight years. She was feisty, which was necessary for her to survive in a work world that was male-dominated and full of sexism. "It was a huge learning curve for me—coming from Truro, where everyone knows everybody and everyone's your friend, to this world of, 'Oh God, I just want to screw you,' and married men showing up to your barracks door, removing their ring and wanting to sleep with you."

And yet somehow, she managed to put up with the bad behaviour and take it in her stride. "Best postings I ever had was as a trucker. I had so much fun," she says. But the years rolled by and she began to get bored and started looking around for something else to do. She remembers a conversation that confirmed the timely wisdom of her decision to "remuster," the term used to denote being reassigned. A colleague said to her, "Do you know how many times I was in an office and the bosses would have discussions about how they were going to break you? They would proudly talk about it in front of me. And I don't get that." "Because you are a dude," said Shirley. She adds that it wasn't just gender that seemed to provoke animosity from her bosses, it was because she was "smart, Asian, female and a lesbian." Shirley says, "I've got all strikes against me."

Shirley applied to Intelligence in 2002. In her first posting in Winnipeg, she was given a troubling assignment by a supervisor who dumped some gruesome research on her. "He had me look up some information that was not very pleasant. I did, and afterwards he said, 'I'm glad it's you who looked it up. I didn't want to.'" She can't say what it was, but she feels he had deliberately subjected her to difficult material. When the senior officer in charge of their unit found out, he blew his stack and apologized to Shirley. But damage had been done. "I had to learn how to deal with it, and I did," Shirley says. The impact of that experience would haunt her and leave a deep imprint in her memory.

Her second posting was seven months in the United Arab Emirates at Camp Mirage, a once-secret installation in the desert. Because it was a clandestine operation, she couldn't tell anyone where she was going or any details about the briefings that she was doing for aircrew flying from there into Afghanistan. During this tour, the losses were significant; twenty-two people died. "The first female killed in combat was during our tour. I'd say probably half the guys that got killed in Afghanistan were people I knew," Shirley says. She itched to "get outside the wire," meaning outside the secure confines of the military base. "I lost so many people, I wanted to be in the shit. I wanted to kill a few guys to get back." But she began to see that as a member of the drone team she was already inflicting significant damage. "I realized the job I was doing was even worse. I could see everything in detail. You're nothing but the big trigger and it hits you, after, that you are part of people dying. We're all part of that kill, and at the end of the day, whether they're bad people or not, they're still a person."

The stress of what she was seeing and doing had a cumulative impact on her, but because of the secrecy surrounding her work, Shirley can't be explicit about what it was she was experiencing. And she wasn't the only casualty. "The mass corporal I was working with—we actually went through trades training together—made it on the news for throwing himself and his wife off the twenty-second floor in Toronto." In the wake of that tragedy, one headline read, "Robert Giblin, soldier in Toronto murder-suicide, had PTSD, obituary says."

In the fall of 2006, she came back to Ottawa, where she was assigned to the Afghan Intelligence Response Team (AIRT) as a collator. The soldiers who work in Intelligence have been described as "information slingers," and as a collator, Shirley turned research into intelligence that could be analyzed, put into reports and sent to the soldiers on the ground. As she moved up the ranks in Ottawa, Shirley was determined to avoid the missteps of the supervisor she'd had in Winnipeg. When she became chief collator, she insisted that she see difficult information before any of her junior staff. "I didn't want them to go through what I went through," she says about protecting her staff from traumatic material. "I got exposed to some horrific stuff and I made sure that they didn't see it. Some things are better left unseen." But for Shirley, what had been seen couldn't be forgotten. Each instance of exposure inflicted damage to her psyche, like invisible bricks piling up around her.

In March of 2011 Shirley finally got her wish to go to Afghanistan. She was deployed to Kandahar as an intelligence analyst working in the drone program. From the first day she arrived, everything was full-on. Personnel were crammed into a bunker that wasn't big enough for everyone, and on night one, there was a rocket attack that, she says, "shook us out of our racks." Shirley hadn't yet been issued her weapon, which left her feeling exposed and undefended. She feels that "as a soldier, when you know you can't defend yourself because you don't have a weapon, that affects your psyche." She remembers rocket attacks shattering, over and over again, any calm there was on the base in Kandahar. Even their final medals parade was disrupted. Shirley remembers everyone dropping to the ground, in formation, lying there long enough to wait out the attacks plus an extra two minutes to ensure there wasn't another rocket coming. "You don't realize, until after, the effects of constantly getting rocket attacks and not being able to sleep. If it's dark and quiet, I have to have a TV on in my room, because the light prevents the darkness," she says. And she admits she leaves the television's volume up, tuned to the cooking channel, so if she wakes, she hears the sound of English-speaking voices.

Shirley was in Afghanistan for four months, and when she got back to Canada, she began to suspect she was experiencing PTSD. "I remember I was going for my medical and I said, 'I got exposed to some shitty stuff and it kinda had a negative effect on me.' So they sent me for a mental health assessment," she says. Shirley was seen by many doctors, but during one assessment at an operational stress injury clinic, she remembers asking her mental health doctor, whom she affectionately refers to as "cuckoo," how she would assess Shirley's well-being. The military measures PTSD numerically, and her doctor said she was probably 75 percent affected, which is extraordinarily high. That doctor said that Shirley was one of the angriest people she had ever treated, but added that she'd also never seen anyone work so hard to get better.

Sleep deprivation is often used as a form of torture, but when Shirley was in the field it had the opposite effect. She became hyperfocused and calm, so much so that later, one of her doctors would ask if she had been trained as a sniper. However, there would be real fallout from months of being jarred awake by rocket attacks, and it began to show up when she got home. "People didn't believe me that when I got back from Afghanistan, I was only sleeping an hour, or an hour and a half a night," she says. Nighttime was debilitating, because she began having terrifying nightmares.

In its early stages, Shirley managed to conceal her PTSD symptoms from the outside world. "When you're good at hiding shit, you do it in a very strategic way. I was very good at it. People had no idea how much I was struggling," she says. "Few people have seen me lose my shit. I'm a master of disguise. When post-traumatic stress got really, really bad, I bunkered. I just shut people off." Shirley dissolved friendships, withdrew from the world, and stopped talking to her family. She distanced herself, with the macabre intention that "they wouldn't have to blame themselves" if she took her life.

It was Shirley's workmates who figured out she needed a dog in her life, and they started sending her pictures of rescue pups that needed a home. They were just in time, as it turned out. On May 8, 2013, Shirley went into meltdown. She was teaching a course at the base in Cold Lake, Alberta, when a captain cracked a joke about something Shirley had said. "I lost it, and I visualized killing him. I couldn't calm down," she says. Shirley called the social worker on the base and explained what had happened, and the social worker told her to come in straightaway. "I was literally red with rage, and it took two hours to calm me down," Shirley remembers. The social worker sent her home for the rest of the week, telling her she was suffering from post-traumatic stress. Coincidentally, Shirley had already made plans to drive to Lloydminster that evening to adopt a little dog named Snoopy. She made the trip and brought Snoopy home—a twenty-five-pound Pug/Schnauzer/terrier mix with grey and black grizzled hair and great big ears. Snoopy had no special training, she just needed to be rescued. Shirley knew nothing about support dogs, and she says, "I was as ignorant as everybody else about service dogs." Shirley is forthright about how fortunate she was when this funny-looking little mutt became hers. "I knew I was not doing well, and I can honestly say that if I hadn't gotten her that week, I never would have made it through."

It was only a matter of hours before Snoopy's ability to help Shirley was put to the test. "That first night I had a night terror," Shirley recalls, "and I couldn't calm down. She came over, and she put her head on my right shoulder. She wrapped her legs around my arm and stayed up the whole night." Remarkably,

Snoopy instantly understood how to calm Shirley so she was able to fall back to sleep. Snoopy has learned that nudging Shirley and cleaving to her makes bad dreams unlikely to become nightmares or, worse, night terrors. "I can always tell how restless I am by how closely glued to me she is, how much bed she has compared to me. If I'm on the edge and she's got the rest of the bed, I know I've had a rough night."

Shirley has what she calls "daymares" too. "Basically, what I have going on twenty-four hours a day is instant replay of all the different things that have affected me," she says. Sometimes sounds will set Shirley off. For instance, while teaching a course in a building next to an airfield, a nearby aircraft caused a big boom and she was instantly triggered. In her mind, she was lost in Afghanistan. Snoopy helps her in these moments. "She knows I'm struggling before I do. She'll come up to me and start giving me kisses, she'll nibble on my hands, give little love nibbles, so it breaks my thought."

Dogs are considered to be highly empathetic, and keen observers of human body language—many have an innate ability to understand a human's tone of voice, facial expressions and body language, which helps explain how, even without having been trained, they are able to assist humans when they are struggling. There were times when Snoopy helped other people too.

Shortly after Snoopy arrived, Shirley took her in to work to introduce her to the guys. Her captain commented to her that he could see, almost overnight, that Snoopy was having a tremendously positive impact. He told Shirley to continue to bring the dog to work with her, and to do whatever it took to get her trained as a service dog. Shirley began researching training programs, and after numerous false starts with organizations that either wanted to charge her a lot of money and/or give up her dog and take one of theirs, she found George Leonard and Courageous Companions. She applied and was accepted, although Snoopy was much smaller than any dog George had trained before.

Shirley undertook her end of the training at home and in earnest. "I know how to follow direction and listen to subject-matter experts, so everything he said to do, I did, to the letter." When it was time, they went to Winnipeg so George could assess Snoopy. He took them to malls and other public places where Shirley would be confronted by crowds of people. He was impressed with their relationship, and Snoopy passed her certification brilliantly. When George commented on the bond between them, Shirley said, "Yeah, she's my hero, man. Saved my life." Snoopy had earned the right to a vest that would identify her as a support dog, but she was so small that the only vest that fit was a prototype designed for a puppy. George loaned it to her and Snoopy became number 89—the eighty-ninth dog George had tested for Courageous Companions.

From that time forward, Snoopy has been beside Shirley's side day and night. "I teach and I had one of her beds put behind the podium, and at the end of each class we'd get up, she'd go for a pee, come back in, lie down and wait until the next break," she says.

When Shirley got Snoopy, both she and the dog were heavier than they should have been. The vet made no bones about the fact that the dog needed to lose some weight. "The vet looked at me, and I said, 'I know but look at me! We're a perfect match. Give me a month to get her weight down.'" Shirley began walking with Snoopy, five kilometres per day, and the two of them dropped some pounds and are in better shape than ever. "Trust me, the first time we walked five kilometres, it was two hours because the two of us were so out of shape!"

Getting some exercise has helped in many ways, and Shirley's been given specific advice by her social worker to take the dog whenever she's becoming riled up. Most of the time, it helps defuse the situation. Snoopy has other ways of helping Shirley with anger management. One day, during a frustrating visit to a local bank with a friend, Shirley was losing her cool. "Snoopy knows when I'm getting really mad," explains Shirley, "so she dragged me out of the fricking bank. And when I thought I was ready to go back, she's like, 'Nope, you're still pissed off,' and wouldn't let me go back in the bank. When I calmed down enough, Snoopy let me go back in the bank."

There have been some close call moments. There is a political maxim, One Struggle Many Fronts, that could be applied to dealing with PTSD. Once, when Shirley was stressed and felt she wasn't getting the right support around an issue at work, she snapped. "I was actually headed to the airport," she says, "and I was going to ship Snoopy off to her godmother, and I was going to take care of business on the base," meaning she was going to end her own life. Fortunately, her team of health-care providers had intuited that Shirley was in a dangerous place. "My doctor was smart enough to realize what happened, and what probably saved my life was the fact she didn't call the military police or the RCMP, she called my social worker. And my social worker talked me off the ledge." Shirley is still officially a member of the military, because of a deal she made. "It's an agreement I made with my social worker, because as long as I wear my uniform, I won't dishonour it," Shirley says, adding that her sense of duty extends to Snoopy. "My responsibility is to make sure that her life is nothing but the best I can give her."

Since that time, Shirley has become a trainer for Courageous Companions, and she is devoted to George and the work he is doing with dogs. "George is like my brother. There's nothing I wouldn't do for him. I'm alive because he helped me with my dog, and to me, you can't put a price on that." This dovetails with values she learned as a child. "The way my parents brought me up was to always be grateful for those who have helped you. He's a very, very humble man. And that's another reason why I like him." As a trainer, being in the company of others who are struggling with PTSD brings her some unique rewards. "You don't have to explain what you're thinking. You don't have to explain what you're feeling. You don't have to explain the hypervigilance and how you react to certain things."

One of Shirley's social workers once told her, "When you look at your dog, or you talk about her, everything about you softens. There's no mistaking the love you have for her." Shirley is massively better off since Snoopy arrived in her life. "Honestly, I would not be alive today if wasn't for her," she says. But she's also pragmatic about where she's at, saying, "I'm still working on it. I'm still a work in progress."

Krypto

Krypto's Fire

When five-year-old Clarke got his new Sheepadoodle puppy, he named him after the canine sidekick of Superman, his favourite superhero. Krypto, a black and white ball of fur, earned his superhero moniker when he was just eight months old and saved the lives of his entire family.

Clarke and his parents were tucked in for the night in their home in Stratford, Ontario. Clarke's dad, Kyle, remembers stirring, smelling smoke and drowsily wondering who would be having a campfire at that time of year. But he thought no more of it and went back to sleep. At about 11:30 p.m., Kyle was awakened by Krypto, who kept nudging him and licking his face. The pup had never done this before and was so persistent that Kyle got up to see what was afoot. When he looked out the bedroom window, the back of the house was glowing red, and he ran downstairs and found chest-high flames licking up the side of the house. Kyle tore back upstairs to the second-floor bedrooms where Clarke and his mother, Jackie, were sleeping and shouted to them to call the fire department. He ran downstairs and began hosing down the fire, while Jackie made the call and decamped to the neighbours' with her son and the dog. By the time the fire department arrived, Kyle had all but extinguished the blaze, though the fire department doused the deck and exterior walls to ensure there were no smouldering embers.

Everyone was shaken by how narrowly they had escaped catastrophe. When Kyle and Jackie surveyed the damage in daylight the next day, they were horrified to see that the fire had melted the vinyl siding on the second floor of their suburban house and scorched the brick on the first floor. It was a close call. Jackie says the fire chief who attended the blaze told them that if Krypto hadn't alerted them when he did, they could have lost the entire house. Worse still, they could have died in the fire. Flames were minutes aways from getting into the attic and igniting the roof timbers, and they had spread to within a couple of feet of a gas line that led into the house.

When firefighters ripped off part of the deck they found the culprit—a grease trap hanging underneath the natural gas barbecue. Hot grease dripping out of the overfilled trap had made its way down between the boards of the deck and into dry fall leaves. Jackie says the firefighters told her the leaves may have smouldered for some time, waiting for the right conditions to combust into a full-on fire.

The impact on everyone was dramatic. "It really was scary. Clarke was traumatized—so much so that later that night he threw up from the adrenalin. He's had a bit of anxiety since, not wanting to sleep in his room," says Jackie. "I was also full of adrenalin. Your mind goes into the 'what ifs'. What if we didn't catch it? What would have happened? But thankfully we did."

Kyle remembers how frightening it was to see just how close the fire had come to his son's bedroom window.

It is not uncommon for dogs to react to fire and smoke. Krypto's reaction to the fire is, in part, explainable by a dog's innate sense of smell—from the moment they are born it is 100,000 times more sensitive than that of humans. Dogs also have an excellent sense of hearing, and a thermal sensor at the tip of their noses that makes them very sensitive to even minute temperature changes. These factors may help explain how a young and untrained puppy knew something was wrong. What they don't explain is why the pup knew enough to pester Kyle until he woke in the middle of the night. However, on that October night Krypto did, and he became the family's protector, a canine smoke detector!

Penetrating Silence

When Marilyn slipped in a puddle of water on the bathroom floor, her husband Larry was oblivious to her cries for help, even though he was on the other side of the door. Larry is deaf, and this accident was his worst nightmare. *And hers*. She had really hurt herself, striking her jaw on the tub as she fell. Larry was mortified that he hadn't known she was in trouble. Knowing that she was lying on that floor made him feel sick. He and Marilyn had worried about disaster scenarios before, and she'd once said to him, only partially in jest, that if she were hanging on for dear life having fallen off a cliff, she could plummet to her death and he'd be completely unaware it had happened—even if he were only a few feet away!

Larry hasn't always been deaf. He lost his hearing while working for three decades in Vancouver sawmills, where he ran heavy machinery. His working world was a cacophony of sounds—whirring and clanging and booming all day long. Nothing could adequately cancel out the intensity or the volume of noise. He had already suffered significant hearing loss by the time he was in his late thirties. Even with hearing aids and a cochlear implant, Larry's hearing became progressively worse, and the deafer he got, the deeper his feelings of social isolation became. He describes the experience as frightening and humiliating. "You don't want to go where there are people, because you're not going to hear them. And if they say things to you and you get it wrong, it's a big ha ha ha, you know? It's like laughing at somebody because they're sitting in a wheelchair and can't walk. I mean, it's the cruelest thing anybody could ever do. And for people who become deaf, this is what happens."

The isolation Larry describes can have serious health implications, like depression and anxiety. But Larry's increasingly circumscribed life had a significant impact on Marilyn too. She is a social butterfly, active in her community and her church. Larry is a genial man, but when they attended a social function together, he would sit by himself in a corner. She'd be torn between sitting with her husband or mixing with the other guests. Larry had grown up in the church; his father was a Salvation Army pastor. From the time he was a youngster he would greet parishioners as they came to services. His ability to interact easily with people was a point of pride. As his hearing diminished, he couldn't do this anymore. Loss was all around him. He couldn't discern what was being said during a Sunday service, and he could no longer enjoy listening to music in the church. Over the years, his frustration mounted. "You lose contact with people, because it's too much trouble and too embarrassing. It's like you are different right from the start."

They managed all these losses, but Marilyn's fall was a tipping point. What had been a worry became a serious reality, and Larry decided it was time to do something about it. He enquired about getting a service dog. He and Marilyn lived on Gabriola, one of British Columbia's Gulf Islands, and members of the community rallied to help. When Larry learned that he'd qualified for a trained service dog at a school in Ontario, he jumped on a plane and headed east.

In some schools, when trainers are assessing which dogs to pair with potential owners, they introduce the dogs and people and watch what happens. In Larry's case, there was one special dog, Vespa, that let the trainers know who *she* wanted. She kept gravitating toward Larry, crawling under his chair when he sat down, laying her head at his feet. From the moment they met, their attraction was mutual, and they became inseparable. When the school decided to formally pair them, they lived together twenty-four hours a day, getting to know each other intimately during the training process. Vespa, a two-and-a-half-year-old Yellow Labrador with gently expressive golden-brown eyes, would change his life for the better and would do the same for Marilyn.

Vespa is Larry's constant companion; she is with him every day, everywhere he goes. She's highly trained to respond to his needs. "You'd swear she understands everything you say," Marilyn says. "I can ask Vespa to go get him and suddenly I'm not screaming, 'Larry, Larry,' like I used to." When Marilyn has prepared dinner, she asks Vespa to get him, and the dog brings Larry to the kitchen, which is particularly helpful because Marilyn has bad knees and walking is tough. Or when they go shopping and end up in separate parts of a busy big box store, Larry tells Vespa to find Marilyn. The dog looks around, gets a bead on Marilyn, and escorts Larry to her. These seemingly simple things do a whole lot to make their lives easier.

Larry's ability to go out into the world has been significantly enhanced since Vespa arrived. When Larry is preparing to go out for a walk, he will say, "Vespa, circle, advance forward and form your line," at which point she gets up, comes to him and stands by his leg, ready for action. If she's in the wrong spot, Larry says, "Back up, back up," until she's in position and he can put on her leash. To praise her while in service mode Larry says, "Good job, soldier." When they are out in the world together, Vespa alerts him to the things he cannot hear—oncoming traffic or an approaching person who is out of sight. By making physical contact she can lead him away from, or toward, a sound.

When something comes up that requires Larry's attention—a doorbell rings, someone knocks at the door, or his cell phone goes off—Vespa doesn't bark; she finds Larry and jumps up. He says, "Show me," and she takes him wherever he's needed. Larry and Marilyn have also trained Vespa to be relentless in her search for either of them. This was particularly useful when Larry locked himself in the garage. He was banging on the door and, hearing the ruckus, Vespa ran through the house looking for him. When he was nowhere to be found, she brought Marilyn to the garage door. An important part of Vespa's safety preparation is how she's trained to respond to the fire alarm. If it begins beeping, Vespa spins counter-clockwise, alerting Larry to this specific danger.

Marilyn says Vespa's comprehension and vocabulary are remarkable—and jokes that it's as if the dog speaks English! "She is like Lassie all over again. This dog has human understanding—it's unbelievable!" Larry has a favourite story proving Marilyn's point about Vespa's acumen. One day they were using public transit on a route that was new to them. Larry boarded the bus and sat down, and Vespa settled under his seat. When Larry asked the driver if they were nearing their stop, the driver indicated yes. Larry issued the command, "Vespa, mount up and advance forward." Then he realized there were more stops to go, and he became anxious that Vespa might fall while the bus was moving. He said, "Vespa, hit the deck, suck up that floor quick, and put your paws on your beak." Even though he was giving a command that contained words he'd never used before, Vespa somehow understood and immediately lay down and put her paws over her nose, much to the astonishment of the other bus passengers.

Marilyn and Larry have been happily married for fifty years and are frank about the challenges and disappointments that they have experienced as a couple. Marilyn says these have put a massive strain on their relationship, and they have lost some of the touchstones that enriched their lives together. Things they used to share, like music, are no longer available to them, because what Larry hears is just tone or indecipherable noise. Marilyn also misses the nuanced communication they used to share. "There's a lot of interpersonal stuff that just went out the window with the hearing," she says. "There are no sweet nothings between us." Yet Vespa opened new lines of communication as a non-verbal go-between, helping renew Larry and Marilyn's bond. When it comes to disagreements and tensions between them, Marilyn smiles and says, "Vespa can sense the feeling between us, and she'll do something ridiculous that leaves us both laughing. She seems to know when to turn it on, like a kid would do to get Mom and Dad back together."

The most profound gift Vespa has given Larry is to restore his confidence around people. "I feel that I'm not alone because I have my buddy with me," he says. "And when I say buddy, she really is a buddy. She is my friend." Vespa reopened the world to him. "He feels connected and even though he can't hear, Vespa is hearing for him. The dog is now his connection," Marilyn says. Tellers and store clerks regularly say how amazed they are by Vespa's devotion to Larry. "This dog never takes her eyes off him. She is locked on him, waiting for every clue, any command. She worships him. 'Anything you need, I'm here. Your wish is my command.'" Marilyn jokes, "She lives only to get up and serve him. I don't live only to get up and serve him!"

The man who used to sit alone in a corner no longer feels isolated. Marilyn says of Vespa, "She has given him independence, but what she has done for me is to bring me peace. I jokingly say she is my sister/wife and honestly, she is. If I died, it would be a great loss for Larry, because I would be gone. But if Vespa died, it would be a greater loss. I handle stuff that he could learn to do and get by, but he and that dog are one." And more than that, now that Larry has his own special companion, he isn't imprisoned in a lonely ghetto of silence. As a result, Marilyn says, "Vespa opened his heart."

Mollie

Diagnosis for Distraction

In the spring of 2020, a few months into the pandemic, Barbara pulled up stakes, piled her stuff into the back of her car, and drove two thousand kilometres across the country. Her destination was a ramshackle bungalow she had bought in the city where she had grown up. Her plan was to test whether life would be easier when she was living closer to her family. Because she is a successful writer, she wasn't worried about her professional portability. "I was the classic COVID cliché. I worked on Zoom like everybody, so it didn't matter where I was, so I went and lived in a little shack on the prairie," she says.

Barbara settled into her new digs, doing repairs, patching holes and painting. But it was tough to be a woman on her own in a new place, especially in winter during a pandemic lockdown.

She had undertaken this adventure solo, but after a while she began to feel a tug from things familiar back in Toronto. "I'm very happily single, but I do get lonely sometimes. Some people have a shyness gene or a bedwetting gene, I have a loneliness gene," she says and laughs. "The whole point was to go and hang out with my many siblings and nieces and nephews. But everyone was so COVID nervous, we'd have picnics in the park at forty below . . . sitting around in lawn chairs playing Frisbee in the cold."

She found herself pining for the company of a dog. When a close friend heard it once too many times, she exhorted Barbara to "just get the damned dog!" Barbara was part of the wave of people seeking canine company during COVID, so puppies were in short supply. "I looked around, couldn't find a mutt for love or money. I thought I'd get a rescue, like a responsible person. Week after week, when I went online it was like the same three or four dogs were available," she remembers. Those dogs had some serious issues so she shifted her focus to breeders, but their litters had also been claimed—until the phone rang, and one of the breeders called her back with good news. "They had extra Labradoodles, and so I chose one from pictures and then drove out and picked up my little eight-week-old puppy, Mollie, and brought her home. She was just a ball of black fluff." Barbara set about training her, and they became, as she says, "super COVID codependent."

Before Barbara moved away from Toronto, she had had some health issues, and when she got to her new home she continued to follow up with local physicians. In the spring of 2022, it was determined that she had stage 4 melanoma. It was a sobering diagnosis, and when her doctors advised that she might be better served by the care available in Toronto, Barbara threw all her stuff into her car and made her way back to Ontario, this time with Mollie in tow.

Barbara began treatment that fall. Her cancer was so advanced that doctors put her on immunotherapy followed by numerous drug trials, and her life became a kaleidoscope of one medical problem after another. Everything made her sick, and even the drugs she took to counterbalance the negative side effects had serious consequences, which meant she was in and out of hospital constantly.

In the midst of Barbara's medical hell, her dog was the bright spot. Mollie is a long-legged Labradoodle, dark brindle in colour and very poodle-like in appearance. She prances, and Barbara is a slender blonde, so when they are together they have the simple elegance of a cashmere sweater worn with jeans. Mollie is constant company for Barbara, who natters to her all the time. "It's like there's someone in your house and you can talk to them, and she moans at me when she wants something or she brings a toy and looks at me like, 'Chase me!'"

While Mollie's needs are a responsibility, and sometimes a burden, she is an endless source of comfort to Barbara. And ironically, the quotidian details of Mollie's care and feeding give Barbara a reason to get out of bed. "Otherwise, I'm too sick to work. I have no one to take care of but myself, so I could easily lie in bed for days at a time. I have people like my daughter and my niece and my friends and my neighbours that look in on me, but with the dog, I have to get up and put my clothes on and go out," she says. "It certainly takes you out of yourself, and it's always very healthy to do that." And when things were at their worst, Barbara remembers the little glimmers that helped her cope. "You can't have a dog and not laugh every day," she says. "I had to laugh through my agony."

When Barbara lost thirty pounds very quickly during one round of treatment, Mollie lost weight too. And while Barbara says she's loath to go down a "spiritual woo woo road," she feels sure that the dog intuited her anxiety. Mollie's reaction to Barbara's anxiety has created some gnarly situations too. "As I lost weight, she got freaked out. She started acting strange in the park, chasing people, which she never did before. We have such an intense one-on-one relationship it's sometimes inconvenient, because we go out and she's just a bundle of anxiety and she barks at other dogs," Barbara says. *And* there have been several occasions when Mollie's reaction to Barbara's misery has played out viscerally. "I had a few sessions of violent throwing up and she threw up the same night. The first time I thought it was coincidence, but after two or three times, it was like, 'Holy shit, she's mimicking me.'"

As a new dog owner, Barbara began to discover a whole new world she knew nothing about. In Winnipeg she and Mollie routinely walked the myriad riverfront trails alongside the Assiniboine, but they were usually doing it alone. In her Toronto neighbourhood, morning and evening walks revealed something else—an unanticipated sense of community with people from outside her own circles. "I've lived in this neighbourhood for forty years and I suddenly made friends in the neighbourhood. All my friends before were journalism people; I didn't know 'normal' people like doctors, lawyers and plumbers, I only knew other journalists," she says.

While she and her new friends dawdled in the park morning and evening, they made a kind of small talk that is surprisingly easy to manage. "It's the kind of relationship where you don't have to email or make a date or change the plan six times. You just go and they're there. We text each other sometimes if it's too rainy or too muddy, or we're not going to show up—or we just take our chances." She became especially connected to two of the regulars, Philip, the owner of a Shiba Inu named Vakka, and David, whose dog Barbara describes as a 130-pound mongrel Wolfhound/Newfoundlander mix, named Fiona. Their triad became very special to Barbara. "David is like the ringleader. He is this tall, jovial, funny, great guy who just includes everyone," she says. She describes how the park dynamics change when he's not around. "You know when the mother duck goes underneath the water and the ducklings lose their formation and go around in circles? That's what the dog park is like when David's not there. He's the leader." Just as Barbara appreciates their camaraderie, so, too, does Mollie treasure her new dog buddies. "When they are away or they don't show up, I go to the park with Mollie, and she just sits beside me and looks for them. She won't play with any other dogs, she won't run around, she's afraid to take her eyes off the street they're coming from. And we both just sit there like statues at the dog park."

Barbara's attachment to her two new acquaintances deepened when she was knocked over by some roughhousing in the dog park one day. She was in a weakened state from treatment, and when she fell, she broke two ribs. She couldn't get up, so David came to her aid and picked her up, and not yet realizing the full extent of Barbara's illness, joked about it with her. When Barbara subsequently confided the gravity of her circumstances to Philip, all joking was set aside. Before Barbara knew it, David and Philip were stopping by her apartment building to check on her, often bringing her fresh-squeezed orange juice and other treats. These friendships, facilitated by Mollie's presence, became another lifeline. "I shudder to think that if I didn't have this dog, I never would have met these people," Barbara says.

When first asked whether she felt that her dog had saved her life, Barbara said she didn't think so. But, a year later, her response is different. "I've had nights and days over the past year where I thought, 'If I didn't have this dog, I'd be out of my mind,'" she says. "Before I wouldn't have said that Mollie saved my life, but now I think I could, because I've come out of two years of just absolute brutal treatment, and I'm physically feeling better but I'm mentally crashing." It is ironic that the fast lane of one treatment after another kept her so busy, and so unwell, that she didn't have time to reflect on her circumstances. "When you're getting treatments, you just forge ahead. You have lots to do, your schedule is full of doctors and tests and this and that. Now it's anticlimactic, you know?"

One thing Barbara regrets is that she hasn't been able to take Mollie with her when she goes for treatment. "If I could bring my dog, it would just be huge," she says. "Just scratching her, rubbing her, petting her—it's like worry beads or something. It's this insane resource of this thing you can just touch. They love it, and you love it. It's an endorphin exchange. When I'm at the hospital, I always wish she could be there with me. I think it would help me so much."

Barbara is pragmatic about what is ahead of her. "I'm in a very useful compartmentalizing denial about it. I feel like we're all in the same boat, but I just have more information about how I might go," she says. "I don't know when that might happen. I'm not in a hospice, I'm not dying, but now I feel really depressed."

To cope with the mental crash she describes, Barbara has opted to take antidepressants. She's not sure how well they're working, since depression ebbs and flows, and the meds don't change the reality that she is most likely in a palliative stage of her illness. Barbara's doctor let slip recently that she has outlived her original prognosis, which was one year. She remembers her reaction being "'What? Nobody told me that! Shit. I was supposed to die a year ago?"

"I feel like I have to keep going for my dog's sake, because I don't have anyone to give her to," she says, laughing. "I feel like no one will love her as much as I do. I feel this way about my daughter. There was a day in my daughter's childhood where I was crying because no one would ever love her as much as I would; I wouldn't be here forever and what a tragedy. And now I feel like that about my dog. I know it's neurotic. I laugh at myself. But I just have to find the right home for her before I give up the ghost and get ready to succumb, whenever the time comes to do it."

And Barbara is succinct about that. "Without my dog, I don't think I would have lasted this long. I think I would be sicker, and I think I might even have given up sooner. Like MAiD [medical assistance in dying], bring it on," she says. "I would say Mollie's been a godsend."

Foreman

First Responder

Sinéad is a whip-smart thirty-two-year-old who loves to crack wise—but it's a wonder she has any sense of humour at all, because she is in chronic pain and her body is constantly breaking down. She was born with an extraordinarily rare congenital condition, Parkes Weber syndrome, which affects only eight hundred people worldwide.

Sinéad's vascular, muscular, lymphatic and skeletal systems are all compromised. She has arterial malformations in her right leg and foot, which means a group of blood vessels are formed incorrectly and can cause uncontrolled bleeding. Sinéad remembers one morning she noticed a spot of blood on a bandage she'd put on her foot for a small cut. She felt a pulsing in her foot, and when she took off the bandage to investigate, blood flooded the bathroom floor.

In Sinéad's case, even the smallest cut, scrape or bump is potentially fatal. Some of her wounds do not heal. She has recurring infections that require intravenous antibiotics, and heart issues that can cause dizziness and, at worst, heart failure.

Sinéad was an athletic child, but in her early teens her health began going steeply downhill. Doctors told her she needed to rest and she had to give up her beloved sports. It took years to figure out what was afflicting her, and she was repeatedly misdiagnosed. Most of her young life was spent in blistering pain. When she was in grade 8, her skin began to disintegrate and she developed open wounds that wouldn't heal. Skin grafts and heavy antibiotics didn't help. After a year on bedrest, inactive and frustrated, she became increasingly isolated, which was tough on her mental health.

Parkes Weber syndrome also causes the bones and soft tissues in one limb to overgrow, making one limb longer and larger—in Sinéad's case, her right leg. When it swells it gets heavy with extra fluid and she must use a walker and, at times, a wheelchair. As a young teen, her mobility was compromised by a hole in her foot that did not heal for more than a decade and was so painful she couldn't wear shoes, making it difficult to walk.

Even though she has had to figure out how to handle anxiety, depression and PTSD, Sinéad has a wide smile that lights up her face, and she laughs a lot, sometimes with the help of a broad stroke of sarcasm. She and her brother, Liam, who is four years older than she is, were adopted by their parents, Rita and Gord. Luckily for Sinéad, Rita was an emergency room nurse in an inner-city hospital, and her skill has been invaluable with her daughter's complex health needs. The family lives in a suburban area on the edge of a very large city, and Sinéad has a basement apartment in her parents' house.

In 2014 Sinéad got her first canine help in the form of a tiny puppy named Paddington, an eight-week-old Standard Poodle.

She had hoped he would help her be more mobile, especially when she was trying to make her way around the outside world while using her walker or wheelchair.

Paddington wasn't a trained support dog, but from the get-go he had an intuitive sense about what Sinéad needed. He would cuddle up to her right leg with the wounded foot, and Sinéad remembers her surprise when her foot healed after Paddington had been lying on it for several weeks. Whatever Paddington's canine magic was, the wound in her foot closed over when no medical interventions had worked. In fact, her health began to improve so much that, over the next few years, she avoided dozens and dozens of hospitalizations.

Paddington's temperament, however, wasn't suited for the kind of training necessary for a service dog, although he remains a beloved member of Sinéad's household. She began looking for another dog that was a better fit. Because her needs are so complex, dog schools told her they couldn't adequately prepare an animal to help her. But in 2018 she found a high-level dog program in Winnipeg that usually provides dogs for veterans and first responders with PTSD, and they agreed to find a dog that could be trained to help with her mobility, perform tasks for her, and manage emergencies if her body goes into crisis.

On Remembrance Day 2019, she flew to Winnipeg to meet her new dog, Foreman. Half Golden Retriever, half Chocolate Lab, with a glossy black coat and brown eyes full of soul, he's smaller than the average Lab, but built like a minitank, Sinéad says, "and when he wiggles his butt he could easily knock you over."

It was love at first sight for Sinéad; from the moment she got there, they began to work together to make sure they were a good fit. Foreman leapt into his tasks. He intuitively knew to be careful around her very fragile leg and foot. "When my leg gets swollen, I can't even reach my foot, I'm in too much pain. It's like he knows that he must be really gentle, so he'll just take a little bit of sock, take a little bit, take a little bit and then pull the sock off. I didn't teach him that. Nobody taught him."

Foreman has many skills. He can retrieve things, open and close cupboards, get water from the fridge. "He loves doing laundry. Sometimes I turn it on, but if I'm really lazy, I will make him turn it on. He can open doors, hit the buttons for doors. He picks things up. That's a huge thing because I get dizzy if I bend over too much."

Perhaps most important is the medical assistance Foreman provides. He sleeps with Sinéad, although he's a bit of a bed hog, she says, and even tends to take over her favourite pillow. Some nights she wakes to find herself scrunched up on the edge of the bed. The upside is that if she has any kind of crisis, he's right there to wake her up. Bleeding escalates so quickly that she could be in a dire emergency before she even knows it, and when that happens, Foreman will get her phone and an emergency kit and bring them to her. Or if she is completely unaware of a bleed, Foreman may see or smell her blood. "If I'm dead asleep and he's sleeping, because dogs don't sleep the same way we do, he'll wake me up. The hardest part is not freaking out about it, because then you bleed more. Now I have this whole kit with tourniquets and gauze, everything. I have dog pee pads in there because I put on a tourniquet and then wrap the pee pad around my foot to at least contain it a bit." Then Sinéad goes to the hospital, where trained staff can staunch the bleeding. Foreman is also trained to do deep pressure therapy and lie across Sinéad's body to calm her nervous system if she gets anxious or upset.

Foreman has literally saved her life numbers of times since they became a team in 2019. His nose, with 300 million scent receptors, helps him detect things Sinéad isn't even aware of like blood clots, spikes in her blood pressure and heart rate, and serious infections. A few years ago, she developed an infection that became septic, a life-threatening medical emergency that requires powerful antibiotics and hospitalization, and it was Foreman who detected it.

When he detects fluctuations in her blood pressure or heart rate, says Sinéad, "he will start being very persistent. He'll start by nudging me, and he'll start licking the inside of my wrist and my hand, really hard," she says. "Then he gets me to sit down. The other day, my heart rate went from 47 to 149. I felt fine, and I'm like, 'What are you doing? Leave me alone.' Then I got really dizzy and I'm like, 'Oh, shit. Okay.'"

Foreman also senses a migraine coming on. Before one takes hold, he begins nudging her, and if she's paying attention and she takes her glasses off, he licks her eye on the side the headache is going to affect. Foreman's ability to anticipate a migraine stems from his strong sense of smell, as changes take place in Sinéad's nervous system and in her breath.

In one particularly dramatic instance, Foreman detected multiple blood clots in Sinéad's lungs. Although she had the hallmark symptoms, she had no idea she was in trouble and could have died that day. "I was like, 'Oh, it's fine. I just have some back pain. Oh, I put on weight so I'm just a little more breathless going up the stairs,'" she says. "He started snipping at my chest and poking me with his nose." She told her home care nurse, who was adamant that she go to the hospital ASAP. Sinéad took the nurse's advice and went to get urgently needed treatment. Foreman went with her, and Sinéad, with some amusement, remembers that while she was on a hospital table being scanned, he couldn't resist being a dog when opportunity presented itself. She thought she'd put him in a "down-stay" position on the floor, but unbeknownst to her Foreman opened the zipper on her backpack, found his treat pouch, and devoured the contents.

Foreman has helped Sinéad find her independence. Before he arrived, she had never been on public transit. She's nervous about being in the company of strangers, and if she becomes anxious Foreman is trained to stand behind her or create space for her. Now she's even learning to drive, which she thought would never happen because of her leg and foot. Thanks to Paddington and Foreman, her foot has been in good shape for more than five years, and if it does open up it heals quickly. Having Foreman, and Paddington before him, has provided some emotional healing that gives a sense of relief to Sinéad and to her parents, because they worry less.

When asked how she manages to remain so optimistic and upbeat despite her precarious health, Sinéad pulls a treasured gift from her bookshelf, and says, "Well, that's because Joni Mitchell said I had to be!" Mitchell, who is Sinéad's hero, inscribed a copy of one of her books after a friend of Sinéad's told the singer/songwriter about her. The inscription reads, "Pain and illness are great but terrible teachers. I have learned much from illness. Find a quiet place within you. Massage your heart chakra. Be as much as possible of good cheer." These words delight Sinéad and she holds them close, as if they are a survival mantra.

Foreman has also brought her joy beyond his role as a service dog. In 2022 Sinéad began to volunteer at the Toronto Zoo, which is just a short distance from her home, and Foreman officially became the zoo's first volunteer service dog.

Volunteering can be a complicated business for the physically disabled, even more so for those who have service dogs, and Sinéad has found that some establishments are less than welcoming. But she is exuberant about how warmly they've been received. And, serendipitously, it has led to an unlikely friendship. A young female gorilla named Charlie took a shine to Foreman from almost the moment she first clapped eyes on him through the glass around her habitat. She comes over to the window and sits with him. She shows him her toys and will tempt him with her snacks. When Charlie is really happy, she spins in circles. Sinéad says, with delight, "We had to be away for a month, and she noticed he was gone and when we came back, she started doing circles!"

Jedi

Jedi Warrior

Kal's broad, open smile obscures a childhood crowded with pain. Now an impressively articulate twenty-four-year-old university student, there was a time when Kal felt their future prospects were dim. Kal (who uses the pronouns "they/them") is autistic, and as a youngster, their world was a confusing kaleidoscope of sounds and visuals that were often "bigger, brighter, louder and more overwhelming" than Kal could handle. Kal wasn't properly diagnosed until they were a teenager. "Growing up I didn't know this was how my brain worked, so I didn't develop adequate strategies or receive support to cope with my needs," they say, adding, "I also have synesthesia, meaning that some of my pathways for sensory information are mixed up. I can *hear* some lights the same way I can hear noise from a speaker."

Kal often missed a lot of school, sometime weeks at a time, but they were able maintain excellent grades, so no one looked too deeply into the reasons. "I was just understood to be chronically ill." Kal also struggled with social skills, which made them an outsider. They remember being a target in elementary school, where they were relentlessly mocked and bullied.

At the age of twelve, Kal was diagnosed with anxiety, obsessive-compulsive disorder and depression. On top of this, Kal has a sensory processing disorder and their brain has trouble dealing with information it receives from auditory, visual and other senses. Their autonomic nervous system can become overstimulated, causing them to have a kind of seizure called a syncope. Their heart rate and blood pressure drop suddenly and they briefly lose consciousness. These seizures last only a few minutes and most people recover quickly, but that's not the case for Kal. Rather, when they come to, they are disoriented and have trouble communicating. Kal has little awareness that they are about to have a syncope episode, and in the aftermath, what little they do remember is foggy. "I was injured frequently from falling, typically with bruises and scrapes, sometimes sprained joints, and once fell downstairs, resulting in a severe concussion," Kal says, adding, "I'm very vulnerable during both the syncope and post-syncope period, and if one happened while I was alone and someone saw the opportunity, I couldn't stop someone from attacking, stealing from or even sexually assaulting me. Because of the amnesia, it's unlikely I'd remember what happened even if any of those did occur."

Kal describes a frightening episode that happened in high school, in the depths of an Alberta winter. "I had walked outside in my T-shirt and jeans (I'm guessing because I was stressed, and cold calms me, but I must have been stressed to the point of impaired decision-making) and had a syncope in the snow. Typically, because they make me so tired and confused, if I wake up alone from a syncope I just go to sleep, and that's what I did that day, oblivious to the danger." Fortunately, Kal was discovered by a staff member, but the possibility of what could have happened had they not been discovered is still disturbing to them. The experience contributed to a sense of apprehension Kal carried very privately, really only confiding in their therapist. "I became very afraid to be anywhere out of the house alone, even just for a walk around the neighbourhood, because I knew if a situation arose that was beyond my capacity, I could be in serious danger."

Another part of Kal's difference had to do with gender dysphoria, which they struggled with throughout their childhood and teenage years. "When I was very young and learning about gender, I knew without a doubt that I wasn't a girl," they remember. "This internal struggle permeated every facet of my childhood. There wasn't anywhere I could hide from it." One painful memory stands out vividly. Kal was to perform at a kids' piano recital but hated their outfit. "I had to wear this atrocious pink frilly dress that not only made me uncomfortable visually but was also a sensory nightmare." Kal remembers screaming and crying in protest, but finally acquiescing and agreeing to wear it. "Accepting my defeat, I slipped it off and put on a T-shirt and shorts underneath," Kal says. "The requirement was that I had to wear the dress for my piano recital, so I did exactly that, and after finishing my piece, as I was walking back to my seat, I tore my dress off."

As Kal got older things began to improve, though Kal was reticent to be "out" about being gender non-binary (not identifying exclusively as male or female). Kal's high school friends were supportive and referred to Kal facetiously as "transgender on the down-low." Kal doesn't remember any specific date when they officially came out. "Maybe it was in university when I began my medical transition or changed my name. But really, I've been telling people who I was since I was three years old. I just didn't have the words to describe it."

On the medical front, it was no wonder Kal was struggling. Even the experts were confounded. Kal remembers seeing a psychiatrist who was made aware of all their symptoms but failed to diagnose autism. "It was like she'd collected every piece of a stained-glass window but didn't put them together to see the picture."

That was until, at age fifteen, struggling with their mental health, Kal began seeing their current therapist. She has been a godsend. It was she who said that Kal displayed many of the hallmarks of autism, something Kal hadn't even considered. "When she suggested it, I think I actually laughed, because at that time I had a very narrow view of autism," Kal remembers—but, surprising or not, the therapist's diagnosis hit like a "tsunami of clarity," Kal says. "Things about my past, like my difficulties making friends, people making fun of me for reasons I didn't understand, and why certain sensory experiences bothered me and not others" began to make sense, and Kal began to understand why being autistic meant they "could do literal rocket science but not feed myself or take the bus."

While it was a relief to finally have someone figure out what was going on, Kal was confronted with the reality that their situation was something to be managed, not fixed, and that presented some sobering long-term implications. Even though they began to avail themselves of assistance that would make life more livable, what they saw on the horizon was not what they longed for. "I had difficulty imagining a future or any independence for myself," Kal says. For a goal-oriented, extremely bright young person, this was tough to take. "The plans that I had growing up, like getting my PhD, getting married, doing some travelling, and just generally being happy were incompatible with my capacities." The emotional fallout was significant. In junior high school, Kal began wrestling with thoughts of suicide.

And then, in 2016, Kal went to a youth camp on Sylvan Lake, Alberta. What could have been a summer adventure morphed into a life-changing experience.

The camp was massive—three thousand campers and eight hundred staff. Kal's mother, Esther, was also there, volunteering. During opening ceremonies Esther was asked to come to the medical tent. "Kal got overwhelmed because it was a lot of noise, a lot of people, a lot of everything, all happening at once. Kal hit the ground and started having a syncope," Esther says. When Esther arrived at the medical tent, one of the camp doctors asked her permission to bring in a dog that was trained to work with autistic kids. Esther said, "Why not, we've tried everything else." Hudson, a Golden Retriever therapy dog, and his handler came into the tent and the handler dropped the leash. "Hudson passes by four other people, including the doctors that were kind of keeping an eye on everything, and goes straight over to where Kal was," Esther says.

Kal was curled up in a tight ball, arms pulled up close to their chest, with a blanket over their face. Hudson went up to Kal's bedside and put his head under Kal's arm, jostled it a bit, and almost immediately "Kal just took their arm and unfurled it and started petting the dog," Esther says. She likens it to watching a hedgehog uncurl from a defensive posture. Esther was so moved to see her child respond so quickly that she began crying. Kal's recovery time was just a matter of minutes, instead of the forty minutes to an hour it normally took. "For the remainder of camp, when there were large events I 'borrowed' Hudson, who lay with me, or on top of me," Kal says, adding that people who'd known them for a long time were amazed by how Hudson helped Kal stay calm in situations they normally couldn't cope with.

The whole experience blew Kal and Esther away, and they came home determined to find a service dog. Kal had to have a dog trained to respond to their extremely complex needs, and they began the hunt. Eventually, through word of mouth, they found MSAR and George Leonard. At the end of 2017, they were matched with a trained female Labradoodle named Hercules. Kal adored her but it became obvious she was too anxious to be deployed as a service dog, so she had to be officially retired in 2019—although she still lives very happily with their family.

In April of that year, Kal was paired with Jedi, a 110-pound dark brown Chesapeake Bay Retriever. It has been a brilliant match, as is evident from the way Kal's face lights up when they speak about him. "I met my gorilla goober Jedi in April 2019 and we hit it off, meeting up frequently for training and bonding"—the latter was mostly enthusiastic fetch followed by expert-level napping together—"until he came to live with me full time in the beginning of July," Kal says.

Jedi is highly adept at reading Kal's body language. Jedi is able to tell, based on biochemical changes in Kal's body, if a syncope is imminent. "He'll frequently come in for 'breath checks,' where he sticks his nose up practically against mine and stays there until I breathe on him," Kal says. "If he picks up on a sign from my breath or something else, he starts pawing at me until I sit or lay down, at which point he lays across my legs until he decides I can get up. I've learned not to argue." But if they do fall, Jedi is big enough to brace Kal, who is five foot eight, and prevent them from a having a hard landing. Once they are down, Jedi rolls them onto their side in recovery position to keep their airways open. "Once I'm stable, he lays down against me and usually licks me while I wake up. I still wake up foggy, but when he's there I know I'm safe."

Kal has two ways of responding to unsettling circumstances—going inward or exploding outward, what they call "shutdowns" and "meltdowns". Both are caused by experiencing sensations, emotions or stress too intensely and being unable to cope. "Imagine a cup half-filled with water. If you, at a constant rate, continue to gently pour water into it, eventually it will overflow. This gradual buildup, for me, leads to shutdowns," they say. "If instead you dump a full bucket over top of the cup, it's still going to overflow, but it's a much more sudden and violent process. This may result in a meltdown."

Kal describes what happens during a shutdown in this way: "I generally curl up and become small physically and non-responsive to my external environment. In this state the fog that disconnects my internal experiences from external becomes especially opaque. My eyes are physically still seeing things (although I tend to stare at one place), and my ears are still physically hearing things, but I can't process any of it. Touch feels very overwhelming in this state," they say. "Non-human animals are the only beings that can cut through the fog, which is one of the ways Jedi acts as a bridge for me. He is something in the outer world I can focus on, to get myself back, instead of getting stuck inside myself."

Going into meltdown, which can be misread as a tantrum, exacts a particularly stiff penalty. "Meltdowns are a terrible experience, and hard to explain to anyone who hasn't had one. When they happen, I don't have control and don't feel like myself, more like an observer watching from outside my body. Even though meltdowns are loud and big, they've never scared Jedi. He runs to me wherever I am and nuzzles into me, providing pressure, until they pass." Part of what Jedi is doing is deep pressure therapy, which calms Kal's central nervous system, reducing the intensity of these incidents. "He's able to de-escalate meltdowns and panic attacks in a way I've never managed by myself or even with other people intervening. He's got a special puppy power."

Kal began going to university in 2018, the year before they were paired with Jedi. They were studying neuroscience, and school was really tough, but not for academic reasons. Kal was in a chronic state of anxiety and having seizures every week, which was made worse because the university required them to have an attendant follow them around, wheelchair in tow, while on campus. Kal felt crowded by not having time alone to regroup between classes, and it was excruciating. "The university, also for legal reasons, required that an ambulance and campus security be called every time I had a syncope, which meant waking up to strangers prodding me, which was both scary and delayed my recovery."

In second year, Kal was able to bring Jedi to school. They still had to have an attendant, but having the dog with them made all the difference and they had many fewer seizures—only one or two a month. They began to flourish, experiencing much more of campus life, joining an LGBTQ+ student organization. During an annual winter games tournament, Jedi, always at the ready, leapt unexpectedly into action while Kal was participating in a relay race. "As another one of my team members crossed the finish line, he face-planted in the snow and Jedi bolted over, tail wagging, and started rolling him into the recovery position because he thought my teammate was having a seizure!"

Before Jedi, Kal's life was circumscribed in a way that was almost suffocating. "I'd have an incredibly different life without him, much lower quality of life without much prospect for the future," Kal says. But now they can see a happier horizon in front of them. "My dad is my biggest support in life, and without him, I wouldn't be able to meet my basic needs. When the time comes, I'll need to transfer to government supports and potentially also having a partner's support. This is a big scary thing, but a lot less scary with Jedi," Kal says.

Even more remarkably, Kal says they haven't been suicidal since the day Jedi came to live with them.

In an unjust twist of fate, in December of 2023 Kal contracted a bad case of COVID. They were in a comalike state for several weeks and are now unable to speak. They communicate by signing and writing. It has also left them with a weakness in their right leg, causing them to walk with a limp. But Kal and Jedi have met the challenge together. "Jedi has shown his adaptability by learning new ways to support my mobility, preventing falls, and working with mobility aids."

Kal puts it in perspective by making a reference to the Jedi warriors of Star Wars fame. "The Jedi Order harnesses the power of the Force to protect the universe. My Jedi harnesses his love to protect me," Kal says.

I think the healing power of dogs has less to do with what they give us than what they bring out in us, with what their presence allows us to feel and experience.

—Caroline Knapp, *Pack of Two: The Intricate Bond Between People and Dogs*

Calvin

Tale End

As I prepared to write the conclusion to this book, tragedy lurked in the shadows. Calvin, my beloved twelve-year-old dog, quite suddenly became very ill and died.

Calvin was a black Ganaraskan Terrier, a newish breed designed to produce therapy dogs with a gentle demeanour and physique reminiscent of a stuffed cuddly toy. Cal and I did almost everything together. He slept on my bed, tucked up close to me. He was a mainstay in my studio while I worked. He kept me company on long car trips and even shared a kayak when we hung out in the wilds of northern Ontario. I adored him and often joked that if there was one man in my life that I could count on, it was Cal. And truly, if ever there was a dog who delivered comfort and understanding to a human, it was he.

His illness began as a problem with his front left foot. Our vet advised that one of his toes would have to be amputated. It wasn't the first time Calvin faced losing a toe—it had happened on his right foot a few years before. We booked him for surgery, but two days before it was scheduled, as he and I were coming into the house from my studio, Calvin had a seizure. Followed by three more.

Over the next few days, we raced back and forth to the vet. After much consultation we were given to understand that something had gone awry in Calvin's brain, and it was probably a tumour. We had a difficult decision to make, but he was a "senior dog" and none of us wanted him to suffer through further treatments that would, at best, buy him weeks or months.

We brought him home and gathered in my living room for a family confab about what to do. Many tears were shed. Our other dog, Bowie, a nine-year-old Ganaraskan, joined us. While my daughter held Calvin on her lap, Bowie became increasingly unsettled, whimpering, licking her tears away and leaning into her on the couch.

As I think about some of the things I have learned about dogs while writing this book, I realize that what happened that evening was an example of canine empathy. I want to be careful not to anthropomorphize his behaviour, but I do think that Bowie was reading the mood of the room, cluing in to the pain my daughter was feeling and doing his level best to make her feel better.

When a person feels stress or fear or anger, their body releases hormones like cortisol and adrenalin, causing their heart rate and blood pressure to rise and producing chemical changes that are detectable in their breath and sweat. Canine noses are so adept at picking up subtle chemical and physiological clues that when a dog's nose tells them something significant, and possibly dangerous, is happening, they react. And as we've seen, this happens *whether or not* they've been trained to detect these changes.

Bowie may well have been sensing all of our distress, but he homed in on my daughter's because his primary bond is with her. It was, in a sense, his "job" to make sure she was all right.

There are numerous examples of this ability in the stories in *How My Dog Saved My Life*. On the "untrained" side of the ledger, Shelagh's dog Eddie sussed out when to comfort grieving students, Oakee intervened when Khiem's mood became dark, and Moishie calmed nervous (or downright distraught) dental patients.

And there are the dogs who have intervened during a crisis and whose actions save their owner's lives—running for help, as Tinsley did for Cam when he crashed into a gully and as Hero did when Alan was on the edge of succumbing to hypothermia after becoming stuck in a muddy ditch. Or as Daisy did when she raced upstairs and woke Keri-Lynn's husband from a deep sleep, alerting him that she had suffered a stroke. None of these dogs had formal training as rescue/support animals. They just "knew" to do something heroic. A few studies have been done to try to ascertain the when and how a dog's loyalty to their owner kicks in, but for the most part, the why of these rescues is a mystery.

On the other side of the ledger, there are highly trained dogs whose vigilant attentiveness saves their owner's lives on a regular basis. There's Rory Michael, who, of the many ways he supports Kitti, knows to bring a first aid kit to her when she goes into a physical crisis, allowing her time to use her inhaler and call 911 if necessary. Or there's Foreman, who is so attuned to Sinéad that he knows she's in trouble before she does and comes to her with bandages and a tourniquet, giving her a chance to get help before she bleeds to death.

We've also met people whose post-traumatic stress is through the roof. Shirley's psychological scars were so deep that she was considering suicide right up to the eve of the arrival of her little mutt Snoopy. Jason had sunk into a trauma-induced cycle of anxiety and depression that was absolutely debilitating, but with Cheyenne at his side he began to heal. Julie wrestled with the fallout from multiple traumas that were so profound she was becoming unable to engage with the public sphere—until she got Chance, who gets her out of situations that are becoming problematical for her.

And there are the dogs who, through their very loving presence, have helped their humans manage dreadful grief. Alex, with Lambchop's help, made her way through the shock and heartbreak of losing her father to a dangerous driver who mowed him down just steps from his home. And there's Fox, the tiny wonder whose outsize presence in Ania's life was a balm as she struggled through the end of a tumultuous toxic relationship.

Then there's Jenna's dog PJ, who does deep pressure therapy. I met Jenna early in the process of doing interviews for this book, and when she told me that she had trained PJ to do DPT for the anxiety and panic attacks she experienced, I was blown away. I subsequently learned that deep pressure is extremely useful for people with PTSD because it calms the sympathetic nervous system, which is responsible for the body's fight-or-flight response. I witnessed this with Tank and Hailey; when Tank pressed into the back of Hailey's legs, I could see that he was doing DPT to calm her in a stressful moment. And I realize that the way that Bowie sat leaning into my daughter when she was so upset about Calvin was an example of how deep pressure can increase serotonin levels, which can make the lucky recipient feel calmer and more relaxed.

The poet W. H. Auden once wrote, "In times of joy, all of us wished we possessed a tail we could wag." Dogs are capable of such unalloyed happiness, it's no wonder they save our lives each and every day in large and small ways. When Calvin used to take his place on the passenger seat of my car as we began one of our many journeys, he'd wag his tail with an infectious show of enthusiasm. And now, while Bowie lounges on the couch of my studio, the moment he so much as catches sight of me looking over at him, his little tail thumps up and down on the cushions. I am always tickled by the pleasure that connection brings to both of us. As I finish this book and I muse on the people who've shared their stories, I really wish I had a tail I could wag to share my joy at their generosity.

Acknowledgements

The novelist Dean Koontz wrote, "Once you have had a wonderful dog, a life without one is a life diminished." I agree and I'm convinced that everyone who shared their story for this book would too. Their remarkable, sometimes astonishing experiences illustrate the magical connection between humans and their canine companions. I can't overstate how grateful I am to each person for trusting me to tell their story in this anthology.

The idea for this book came from Iris Tupholme, the senior vice president and executive publisher at HarperCollins Canada, who believed that the phrase "how my dog saved my life" contained the makings of a book. I learned of the project when my ever-gentle, ever-persuasive editor Julia McDowell called me out of the blue and asked if I'd be interested in taking it on. I had just retired from full-time work and I must admit that I hesitated for a moment. Fortunately, I saw sense and said yes. Julia edited each draft with sensitivity and a deft hand, for which I am indebted. Alison Woodbury reviewed the text with her legal expertise and made consistently astute suggestions. Tilman Lewis brought his meticulous copyeditor's eye to the text, spotting and repairing my mistakes and "misspeaks." The wise Brad Wilson shepherded the book through its final stages and I so appreciate the enthusiasm he brought to the project.

Writing is essentially a solitary process but I am blessed that my friend Jane Mingay was my editorial confidante and adviser from day one of this project. Jane is a dog lover and has a background in science journalism, and her counsel and indefatigable support was hugely helpful to me. My mother, Janet Cochran, was also an early reader and, as she has always done, ensured I tidied up my grammar and sentence structure. Ellen Vanstone, a writer for whom I have huge respect, was generous with her advice whenever I rang her up to ask for some help. And Roslyn Schwartz, author of *The Mole Sisters* books, whose illustrations grace the beginning of each chapter, brought her cheeky visual cleverness to each drawing.

There isn't a day when I don't thank my lucky stars (as my grandmother used to say) for the fleet of wise women (friends *and* family) on whom I count for steadfast moral support and intelligent guidance. Over many months they took me for umpteen walks, made me countless cups of tea, asked me insightful and challenging questions, and humoured my fretting about some part of the text.

When all is said and done, I am always profoundly grateful for the enduring daily support and sustenance I get from my kids, Jake and Maddie, and my son-in-law, Will, without whom I would be a lesser person.

Lastly, a nod to my dogs Calvin and Bowie. On the long writing days, to look up and see them draped over the cushions on the couch in my studio or sitting at my feet, tails wagging, insisting I take them for a walk, constantly reminded me of the ways, big and small, a dog can save one's life.